MUMBAI
NEW YORK
SCRANTON

MUMBAI
NEW YORK
SCRANTON

by

TAMARA SHOPSIN

with photographs by
JASON FULFORD

SCRIBNER

New York   London   Toronto   Sydney   New Delhi

Scribner
A Division of Simon & Schuster, Inc.
1230 Avenue of the Americas
New York, NY 10020

First Scribner hardcover edition March 2013

SCRIBNER and design are registered trademarks of The Gale Group, Inc., used
under license by Simon & Schuster, Inc., the publisher of this work.

For information about special discounts for bulk purchases, please contact Simon
& Schuster Special Sales at 1-866-506-1949 or business@simonandschuster.com.

The Simon & Schuster Speakers Bureau can bring authors to your live event. For
more information or to book an event contact the Simon & Schuster Speakers
Bureau at 1-866-248-3049 or visit our website at www.simonspeakers.com.

Designed by Tamara Shopsin

Manufactured in the United States of America

1   3   5   7   9   10   8   6   4   2

Library of Congress Control Data: 2012032051

ISBN 978-1-5011-3787-7
ISBN 978-1-4516-8743-9 (ebook)

Permissions appear on page 280.

for Melinda, Dad, and Jason

1.

The plan was if I didn't see him, don't leave the airport. That was it. That was the whole plan. It's 1 a.m. The arrivals area is outside under a giant carport. The air smells like burning garbage. I see Jason so fast. It's almost funny.

There are 100 unlicensed cabdrivers waiting for Jason and me to finish kissing. The cabdrivers are sad now, Jason leads us to a little desk out of the way where he prepays for our taxi.

A few of the drivers follow us. They leave when we reach the prepaid parking area. There are rows of modern and vintage taxis. "I hope we get an old one!" I say.

Our cab is not old or new. The interior looks as if an airplane seat from 1980 has exploded. It is upholstered in a crazy patterned fabric everywhere, even the ceiling. I love it.

On the way out our driver stops at the airport gate. He gets out and goes into a little booth. Two boys come up to the car window one on each side. They put their hands out. Jason and I shake our heads no.

I've heard about Americans who go to India and flip out. They give away all they have with them, take out the max from the ATM, and return home changed forever.

The boys just stand there looking at us with wide eyes. They won't leave. I whisper to Jason asking what we should do. "Roll up the window," he says as he rolls his up quick. I follow his lead but my boy sticks his hand on the glass.

The window closes by a hand-turned crank. I can feel the skinny boy pushing down. I'm playing chicken in the saddest James Dean movie ever.

I continue to roll up the window and am about to squish his fingers when he yanks them out. Our driver returns.

The side of the road is lined with crowded shantytowns. Jason holds my hand and suggests I don't look out the window. Jason has wanted to show me India since the first time we met. My sister didn't say don't go. If she had, I would never have come. But Minda made it clear she didn't want me here. She's afraid I'm too fragile for India, that I will end up shitting chocolate milk and come home weighing eighty-seven pounds.

There are no streetlights. I'm frightened. Jason asks the driver why he has turned off the main road. The driver says it is a short-cut. Jason tells him we would rather stay on big roads.

The Grand Hotel

The hotel elevator sings a song when the doors open. Our room is on the top floor. I open the desk's drawer and paw the turquoise and purple stationery with 1960s typography.

Jason has bought me oranges. I eat them all right away.

I take a shower, careful to keep my mouth shut and puffed full of air. I brush my teeth using bottled water. Even wash the toothbrush off with it.

A travel doctor told us never to drink the tap water here. He also prescribed five hundred dollars' worth of medicine to bring. I filled the prescription uptown near his office. The pharmacy gave me four complimentary tote bags. Really nice ones with a lining.

Jason turns off the lights. He tells me there are more oranges in the minifridge for when I wake up in the middle of the night hungry and jet-lagged.

In the middle of the night I wake up and eat all the oranges.

2.

It's early. There are people still sleeping on top of parked cars and trucks.

Taxis and dogs are everywhere. It is dirty, noisy, and loud. The crowds are thick between crumbling buildings battling overgrown trees. Mumbai is hard fucking core. I love it.

I'm overwhelmed and within three hours of walking need a nap.

Jason has written postcards while I slept and wants to mail them.

A beige one-button mouse skips along the street. A little girl is dragging it by the cord like an old pull toy. We turn a corner and the sleepy neighborhood of our hotel ends.

The streets are so crowded. We must hold hands. Jason says we are near the post office. Stalls line the street. A man will wrap your package. He uses a needle and thread, not tape. At one stall you can pay a man to type your handwritten letter. Jason and I lock eyes.

We stop for lunch. The place serves only veg meals. A veg meal is rice served with a bunch of condiments and a few heavily sauced stewed vegetables. It is all you can eat. I doubt I can eat very much.

No forks or knives. It is customary to eat with only your right hand. Jason says this is because people in India don't use toilet paper so the left hand is reserved for wiping. I don't believe him until he starts to make like he is putting me on and I can tell he is not. The fact that we are surrounded by 150 people eating with just their right hand also helps.

We craft letters to friends in between bites. Jason writes because he is left-handed.

The typist follows each line of our letters with an old ruler to keep track while he types. He corrects two spelling errors and "color" turns to "colour." I think it can't get any better, but then he types the addresses on the envelopes.

The post office is huge. There are birds flying inside. The postage stamps are not peel-off stickers. They are not even the lick-and-stick kind I knew as a kid. They are just printed squares of ordinary paper. There are communal pots of paste decades older than me.

Jason read about a performance by a famous Indian clown. A silent clown who is a national treasure. We have no phone or knowledge of how to use a pay phone. So we walk to the theater across town to find out when it is happening.

It has happened already. I am tired again. Jason says it's the jet lag and that I need to stay awake till 10 p.m. We sit in a park and eat oranges. I place the peels in my tote bag though there is garbage in the grass.

I keep almost dropping the scarf from my shalwar kameez. A shalwar kameez is an Indian outfit made up of a long shirt, loose leggings, and a large shawl. Jason took me to buy the outfit in the Jackson Heights section of Queens before he left for South Korea. Sometimes when the shawl falls off, Jason puts it back on. He drapes it across my shoulders and makes it look like a sculpture of the sea. Within five minutes it will be dragging on the ground. I ask if we can buy some safety pins or Velcro. He says that is cheating.

Jason is lugging around his camera. We stop now and then for him to take a photo. He still uses film. This surprises even Indian people who use typewriters.

The dugout

Mumbai Central

Fruit you can peel is safe to consume. A man has a mound of young coconuts. With three quick cuts, he makes a perfect hole for a straw.

We finish drinking and give the coconut back. The vendor halves it with his knife and uses a piece of the shell as a tool to separate the meat from the rest of the shell. This efficiency seems awesome and a bit cruel. He hands us back the shell holding the loose tender meat.

A stone sign reads "Sir J. J. School of Art." Jason leads, as we wander from one room to the next. The compound is old and disintegrating. The place feels once upon a time enchanted. No students or teachers are to be found. The most action we see is a half-finished sculpture of two Greek gods wrestling.

Drawing class

Schoolyard

3.

For breakfast I eat idli, a white steamed UFO made of fermented lentils. It is served with sambar, which I don't use, and coconut chutney, which I do. The idli is fluffy and easy on the stomach.

We visit a currency museum. The museum is free. It costs no money to see money. Old rupees are on display. Bills pressed between Plexiglas are covered with lovely type, signatures, and intricate anticounterfeit patterns.

I see a bill for ⅜ rupee. Today the exchange rate for one rupee is two cents.

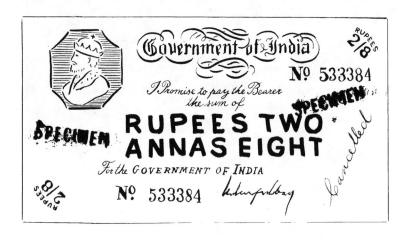

After learning about the history of money, we go shopping at an old emporium. The store is a living museum. The bulk of the merchandise is dead stock from the 1950s. The place has no windows and is dimly lit. This hasn't kept the artifacts from fading. There are more salesclerks than customers.

I browse the racks of shalwar kameezes. There is one with woven purple and black vertical stripes. It has a new-wave attitude and a V-notch neckline. I'm sold.

Poorly lit linens sit in neat stacks behind glass. Jason asks to see them all, one at a time.

The linen lady writes Jason a slip for eight plaid towels and a pink lungi. A lungi is a piece of fabric that a man wears as a skirt. This is Jason's second lungi. He visited India once before, ten years ago, and bought a tan one. Sometimes when it's very hot he wears it around our house.

We hand the slips in and are rung up on an old cash register. Our purchases are waiting, wrapped in paper and string.

THE HINDU

I buy an English newspaper. We sit on a bench and split the paper in half. Jason reads about the threat of Maoist rebels in Andhra Pradesh. I read there is a problem with the motorcycle helmet law. People are just buying crappy helmets off the side of the road.

The helmets don't make crashes any safer. I see a girl drive by wearing a yellow hard hat from a construction site without a chinstrap.

My father rode a motorcycle and would give us kids rides from the small restaurant he and my mom ran. Often the motorcycle helmet was left at home. Afraid of the helmet law, my dad would duct-tape a sweatband to a metal salad bowl for us to wear.

Traffic

We go back to our hotel and order coffee and bottled water from room service. This feels extravagant but it costs less than a dollar.

Jason gave the hotel his laundry to wash. The bellhop brings this with the coffee. Jason opens the package of laundry to find that each article of clothing has an ID tag hand-sewn into it.

Our trip has just begun. We are flying to Cochi early tomorrow morning. Jason organizes his luggage. A bubble jacket and boots are separated out. It is January. He came here from South Korea, where it was full-on winter. There he slept on a heated floor in a traditional Korean house and woke up to snow. It is winter here too, but the temperature is around 80 degrees.

Jason's laundry

4.

The road to the airport cuts through a huge slum.

The airport is clean and modern. We wait for our plane. It feels like a different world. A world with strong coffee and Wi-Fi.

At Cochi airport I climb down the stairs and look for the bus we will take for two minutes. There is no bus. Everyone starts crossing the tarmac to the terminal.

Jason prepays for a cab to the Ernakulam train station while I wait with the bags.

Ernakulam is a lot farther from the airport than we thought. On the drive we see mostly short concrete buildings, billboards, and dust. A friend told me that khaki fabric was invented by a British soldier serving in India who was tired of dirty pants. *Khaki* is a Hindi word that translates roughly as "dust colored."

The train station is confusing, run-down, hot, and dirty. I see real live lepers begging. By the time we figure out where to stow our bags, it's 2 p.m. Time to eat.

We take a scooter-powered rickshaw to an Ernakulam hotel that I read has a great restaurant. Riding in the rickshaw feels just like the Tilt-A-Whirl, only less safe.

Ernakulam

Jason orders the veg meal. He loves it. I get something mushy steamed in a banana leaf. It is very good and comes with a bread called appam. Holy shit, I love appam. It is like idli and a dosa had a fantastic malformed baby. The restaurant is filled with nicely dressed locals, lunching on the same meal as Jason. Across the room a British family is eating eggs and toast.

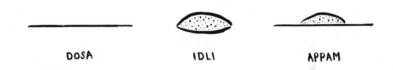

DOSA IDLI APPAM

Fort Cochi is a quick ferry ride from the town of Ernakulam. Most tourists want to stay on the small island with its history, charming buildings, and Chinese fishing nets. I am not so interested in Fort Kochi. I want to see a museum I read about on the Internet.

The museum is called the Hill Palace. It is housed in the old Cochi royal home, located a half an hour away. The plan was to see this museum and catch an evening train. A new plan is needed. The museum closes at 4:30.

Jason and I like this hotel. There are wood details and it feels like 1943. The clerk at the front desk is wearing a suit and asks for our "good name."

Our room is perfect. India is kicking my ass. Jason offers to get the bags from the train station while I nap.

Before the storm

I don't know where I am. I rub my eyes and remember when I see our bags sitting on a 1940s luggage rack. Jason is working at his computer wearing his gingham shirt and a lungi. He is transcribing an interview for a photo blog. The blog is sort of a glorified chain letter. A person interviews you and then you interview someone else who then has to interview someone else. It needs to be finished by the end of the week.

We would normally go to the lobby for coffee, but order room service because it is a dollar.

Jason lets me hop on his computer for a minute to send some e-mails to my family. I send them a photo of me in my India outfit drinking a coconut.

Jason points out that my dad will likely put the picture on the menu. I feel stupid.

My dad used to handwrite the specials on a dry erase board for our restaurant. He would add and delete items weekly with nail polish remover. I still think of his handwriting as smudged capital letters.*

The special boards would get messed up all the time and my dad would throw a shit fit. So I taught him how to use QuarkXPress, one of the first desktop publishing programs.

He would call me in tears at 2 a.m. because he couldn't delete a box. I'd say "⌘K" and he'd hang up. Eventually he got better and stopped calling. The menu grew to six pages—legal size pages.

Now my dad prints the restaurant's menu out daily, adding and subtracting items. He uses gradients, small type, and pictures he finds on the Internet. E-mail from me counts as the Internet.

*With a red asterisk to warn that a dish was spicy.

The bellhop wears a tan uniform. He sets the coffee down in the area of our room I call "the cove." It is a little nook with a window and a loveseat covered in a nubby fabric. Coffee in India always comes piping hot and premixed with milk and sugar. This is good because we can't drink cold milk, but bad because it is always too sweet.

There is a queue of passengers in front of an empty ticket booth. The building feels like a parking garage with no cars. When the ferry docks, a shipmate jumps off and starts selling tickets. As we set sail, he hops back on board and turns into a shipmate again.

Fort Cochin's buildings are nicer than Ernakulam's. The streets are cleaner and lit. The island feels more like Europe than India. Rickshaws pass by and slow when they see us. We wave them off and walk to the restaurant Jason has picked out. The air has started to cool and it feels good.

The restaurant is in a hotel. We go through an arched stone entrance into a tropical courtyard with giant palms and prehistoric plants. To the left and right are covered porches with wicker chairs. Past the garden and porches is the sea. There is a pier with strings of lights hung over tables. We have died and gone to tourist heaven. This is confirmed by the other diners. They are all foreigners like us.

A drop of rain lands on my menu. It is followed by a few more drops. Now a downpour. Jason and I tuck under the covered porch. All the diners have flooded into a small area beneath a tent across the courtyard. Brits are laughing and handling the surprise well. The wait staff is hustling all the tables from the pier into the tiny area.

I tell Jason about the emergency snacks in my bag: cashews, oranges, and two grunt bars (aka energy bars). We run across the courtyard. Jason disappears and reappears with two sodas in glass bottles.

We sit and eat, watching the rain pound the exotic plants while lizards climb the walls. The lights go out for a bit and then come back on.

The rain is not letting up. I stand under the stone arch and watch a taxicab loaded with Brits leave. I wait for the rickshaws to whiz by. They don't. Jason is protecting his camera and asking if a cab can be called. I check the street again. There is one lonely rickshaw. I grab it and call Jason over.

We putter down the little streets that get smaller and smaller till we stop at a house. The driver honks his horn. Rivers flow below us. No one comes. He parks the rickshaw and goes inside. Jason decides the driver is telling his wife that he is taking a fare all the way over the bridge.

There are no doors on a rickshaw. The right side is just always open. Our driver returns carrying a battered tarp. He hooks it over the open side of the rickshaw and we set off again. The roads seem so dangerous.

We cross the bridge, with a man driving a motorbike in front of us. A woman in a full sari is sitting on the back, sidesaddle. She looks totally unfazed.

After a long drive we reach the big road that leads to our hotel. An electrical wire snaps, falls, sparks, no one gets hurt. We pay the driver. He tries to give us change, but we won't take it.

It feels good to be back in 1943. Jason is still hungry and orders room service. We hang our wet clothes over the shower rod. Jason puts on his lungi and works at his computer.

Room service arrives. We sit beside each other in the cove. Jason lifts the silver dome and starts to eat. All the lights go out, including Jason's computer.

We say "Shit!" at the same time.

"Jinx, buy me a Coke," Jason says before I can, and we pinky-swear in the dark.

The lights come back on. Jason's computer doesn't. I unplug the laptop and take its battery out. I let it sit and do all my other computer rituals that have worked in the past.

The laptop starts up. Everything looks fine, then I type: ujkIrfgt sdxciklokjnmrfdeweds plkoyhjufght oklibhjn wsza tfvgwszaed-frnhgbkoplrfded njkmsdfeaweszxds. I type some more and realize the keyboard is adding three extra letters to each letter I type. With the delete key and some patience, a word can be written. Jason wonders how he will transcribe his whole interview this way. I say that we will buy an external USB keyboard. He is skeptical.

Abstract Ernakulam

5.

The hotel breakfast is a buffet. I'm too shy to ask for appam. Jason's not. The waiter brings me some and I light up.

We hire a rickshaw to take us to the Hill Palace museum. It's sunny. The only evidence of the storm is some swaying electrical wires and that the city looks a little cleaner.

The driver points out fishing nets, backwaters, and an elephant along the way.

Tiered gardens lead up to the Hill Palace. The garden is sprinkled with hundreds of potted plants. An Indian couple holds up a camera and asks Jason to take their photo. Jason positions them so they are not backlit and asks politely for a little less smile.

No shoes allowed inside. I take mine off and leave them next to a row of children's sandals.

The shoes are not entirely unprotected.

We find interesting displays throughout the palace, but the architecture of each room is the draw. I walk barefoot on tiled floors and under hand-carved wooden moldings.

The palace is surrounded by historic buildings. One has early rickshaws and carriages. Another has weapons and coins. Yet another has Day-Glo religious sculptures.

It reminds me of the Shelburne Museum in Vermont, founded by Electra Havemeyer Webb. Electra was one of the first people to collect American folk art and architecture. The museum is made up of her collection. Shacks and barns are filled with quilts and miniature circuses.

Electra bought her first piece of art at eighteen. It was a cigar store Indian. Her father was a major collector of impressionist paintings. Buying duck decoys and weather vanes was a teenage rebellion that turned into a lifelong mission. At least this was the sense I got from the biography I bought in the gift shop.

Electra's circus

Behind the main buildings is a short walking path that leads to a life-size fiberglass *Tyrannosaurus rex* and a petting zoo with a snack bar. A swing hangs from a massive tree. Jason holds it still for me to sit. He has me guess what object he liked most. I swing gently and guess it on the first try.

It takes him two guesses to find mine. He gives me a big push that makes me ask for an underdog. "A what?" Jason asks.

I switch places with him and get the swing going really high. I give his back a huge push and run under him shouting, "UNDER-DOG!"

Success.

I catch my breath. Sharp pains shoot through my head. I fold in on myself. Jason comes over and puts his hand on my back. He knows it is a migraine. The headache is gone now. I wait a minute and wipe my tears on my sleeve.

"Oh my God," I say, looking up at Jason, "when I would babysit that would drive the kids bat shit. All they wanted was under-dogs. I got kicked in the head so many times."

Jason created this "get it while you can" rule for traveling. If you like something, you have it as many times as you can. No guilt for not trying something else. I think it originated in Texas when he was trying to justify eating BBQ for every meal. We enact the rule. I order appam with coconut chutney and Jason gets the veg meal.

I enjoy the lobby one last time while Jason checks out.

"The cove"

The only seats left on the train are upper bunks that force you to lie down and have no windows. There is a pictograph sign behind Jason's head. Here is how I interpret it:

1. Do not take snacks from strangers.
2. Snacks are drugged.
3. You will pass out and they will steal your gold watch.

Thrissur is more of a platform than a station. The rickshaw ride to the hotel isn't scary, it is unbelievable. Like a cartoon or an old silent comedy.

The hotel lobby is under construction. The curtains are made of a sheer pink fabric with ruffles. We are the only people staying here.

Thrissur

It's evening. We go for a walk. There is a big roundabout with a Hindu temple in the center. The vehicles zooming around it act as a moat. Jason holds my hand and we make a dash across the road.

We can't go inside the temple because we are not Hindu. I'm glad, temples creep me out.

Close to the temple is a tent holding an ayurveda expo. Ayurveda is an ancient form of medicine in India and a new-age medicine everywhere else. The expo has a fuzzy PA system. Applause and snippets of Hindi escape. There are fluorescent strip lights in the trees. We linger a little and drink a coconut, sitting on some rocks beside a young family doing the same. Across the moat I see a supermarket.

I need to replenish my emergency snack bag. Stationery stores and supermarkets are like wormholes to us. We emerge an hour and a half later with cashews, water, oranges, party favors, a magnet, and a melted Kit Kat.

6.

Morning. The idli at our hotel is the best so far. It comes with an
English newspaper full of articles about Indian movie stars.

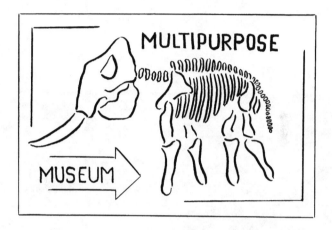

We go to a museum where the exhibits are unfocused. Old tools,
costumes, and botanical specimens sit side by side. The display
cases are beautiful though the contents are falling apart.

It is sad to see this museum disintegrating. There are a few school
groups visiting. I watch a pack of students study a jar of green and
blue slime labeled *baby shark*.

Museum furniture

Vulture

Recent fiction

There is an old chain of restaurants called India Coffee House that Jason remembers fondly from his last trip. We go there for lunch. The waiters wear uniforms that make them look like Punjab from *Little Orphan Annie*.

The town library has a large room filled with men reading newspapers. Jason sits down at the table and joins in. Past the library, a home is being built. It is like watching an episode of *The Flintstones*.

We pass the temple again and head toward our hotel. Giant tour buses are parked nearby. A stage is being made. I don't know what for.

Our hotel room has no windows. At first I thought that was bad. Now I understand it keeps our room dark, cool, and dust free.

Jason wakes me up. It is dinnertime.

There are Christmas lights and scrubby trees overhead. Everyone else is Indian. There is a pleasant din from the tables of families eating and men drinking.

Lettuce here is washed in the tap water we are unable to drink. Which means no salad. This is the food I miss most. Jason points out that there is a side of boiled vegetables on the menu. "Is that safe?" I ask. Jason says it is.

Everything tastes bad to me. Jason loves his meal. He tastes my food and loves that too. It all makes me want to vomit. I don't say it, but he knows. Normally my plate is empty before Jason has eaten half his food.

Jason has tried to teach me manners, but my family put napkins on our laps only if our knees were cold. Jason went to charm school. He grew up in the South and was raised to have faith that everything would turn out okay in the end. I was raised to believe that deep down all people are selfish pieces of shit including yourself and the sooner you face that reality the better.

Jason tells me about the footprints of a Hindu god he once saw. They were tiny, barely the size of a circus peanut. We order sweet drinks for dessert. They are entertaining but we don't drink very much of them.

We leave a bit giddy from the night. Jason tells me I am walking like a drunk person. I laugh and tell him I'm not. He puts his arm around me and guides me up to our room.

7.

Jason paid extra to get the air-conditioned car on the train. Good move. We have a little table and our own window.

Coimbatore is known as the Manchester of India. This is because of its factories not its music scene.

It is just a stopover. We are heading to a place called Ooty. Everywhere in India has at least two names. Ooty is also known as Ootacamund or Udhagamandalam. Everyone calls it Ooty. It's a popular spot for British tourists and Indian honeymooners.

On his first trip to India, Jason took a photo of a viewing platform near Ooty. I decided it'd be interesting to see what it looked like now.

We stop to eat. All they serve is veg meals. It is a prettier veg meal than most and comes with a fried chip Jason likes. I eat just rice. My stomach is upset. I need to use the restroom.

The restroom is Indian-style. It is as if the Hulk ripped the toilet out and all that's left is the plumbing. It makes good sanitary sense because your ass doesn't touch anything. But it's hard to get used to. I have trouble with the multitasking of squatting and doing number two. It makes my head hurt.

Growing up, my three brothers would pee in the kitchen sink. Our family lived in a rent-controlled one-bedroom (aka one-bathroom) apartment. There were seven of us including my parents. I slept on a book shelf. Our restaurant was half a block away. It was like having a duplex with a soda machine.

When I was four my dad was woken up by crying.

The crying was interrupted by a little voice saying, "Nobody likes me. Everybody hates me. I guess I'll go eat worms." The voice waited. "Nobody likes me. Everybody hates me. I guess I'll go eat worms" was repeated and the crying continued.

My parents slept above us in a loft bed that was child-proofed with fishing nets. There would need to be a lot more misery and some blood to get my dad downstairs. Mom would've immediately fumbled for her tie-dyed nightshirt, but she had a gift for sleeping soundly.

From the dark there were footsteps and another little voice. It said, "I love you. I will always love you." And the crying stopped.

My father still can't tell me and Minda's voices apart. I don't remember any of this, but I am sure it happened. Sometimes I imagine me and my sister hugging in the dark with our little arms.

Jason gets seconds of the main vegetable dish, which is five peas in a brown sauce. The waiter asks if I would like more rice.

Ooty is on top of a mountain. It is a three-hour drive. We were supposed to take a bus, but I have turned out to be a wuss. Jason hires a private taxi.

There are hairpin curves and falling rocks. Monster tour buses meet us around each bend. All along the drive are monkeys. Not the cute or magnificent kind. The sneaky ones that try and snatch emergency snacks.

The taxi drops us off at our hotel. It is in a gated compound. Colonial buildings surround a large lawn with a croquet set, bonfire pit, and life-size chessboard. It feels ridiculous.

Upon entering the lobby we are served a lychee spritzer. Jason deals with the paperwork, while I sit on a couch and slurp. I'm not feeling well.

A bellboy brings us to our room. Jackpot. We have a little cottage with a fireplace. Jason uses his computer to send some e-mails despite the broken keyboard. I lie down, thinking I will get back up.

Jason wakes me. He needs to rent a motorcycle so we can drive to the viewing platform in the morning. I ask him to do it without me. After he leaves I puke a few times.

Jason wakes me up. He has rented a motorcycle from a ten-year-old boy and has stories to tell.

Ooty is up on high, which makes the weather cooler, especially at night. This fact doesn't really matter. There is nothing that would prevent us from lighting that fireplace. Jason calls the front desk and they say they will send a boy to light it immediately.

A fifty-year-old man arrives with some logs and lights the fireplace. He resembles an astronomy professor I loved in college. I am snug in bed. It's barely 6 p.m. Jason explains to the man I am not feeling well.

Jason stokes the fire and orders room service. I'm stuck in the bathroom. I can't stop puking.

There is a knock on our cottage door. The man has brought me two hot water bottles with embroidered covers. They look like props from *Little Women*.

I have two thoughts. 1. Wow, that is so sweet. 2. How often does this happen that they have multiple hot water bottles at the ready? Everyone told us, "If you go to India it is inevitable that you will get sick." We are halfway to tautology.

I can't eat the soup I ordered. It tastes awful. Jason has finished his coconut curry. I have not made a dent. Jason seems miffed and says he is going down to the gas station to buy me some plain biscuits that I will eat.

Jason wakes me up. He is back from the gas station. He's not miffed anymore. He has a huge bag of stuff. We lay everything out on the bed. All kinds of cookies and crackers, a nice bunch of postcards, juice boxes, soda, an old wrapped bar of soap, and something called Zandu Balm. The packages and snacks make me feel better. We write postcards by the light of the fire.

8.

Breakfast is held in a wood-paneled room from another era. There are three large buffet tables of food labeled: Indian, British, and Healthy. My eyes light up at the last table. White bowls of blanched green beans, fresh fruit, and cereals. There are no sauces. Nothing is stewed, fried, or overcooked. I fuel the fuck up and eat three meals' worth.

I spend fifteen minutes watching everything I have just eaten go down the toilet. Cornflakes, an English muffin, honeydew, pomegranate seeds, and more. I wash my face and wonder if I should call a doctor. Jason remembers he has Tums in his dopp kit and gives me some.

Jason's earliest memory is of his dad replacing his blankie with a football. At age six Jason was the youngest person ever to run the Peachtree Road Race. His father would lap him as they trained. "Hi jogger!" Jason would say every time his dad passed.

Jason is sitting on the bed quietly with his helmet on his lap. I fill my bag with some of the cookies and juice boxes. "These Tums are working, let's go," I say as I kiss him on the little bald spot at the top of his head.

My helmet is too big. I look like a bobble-head doll. Jason gets the bike started and I hop on the back.

We don't know the name of the viewing platform. There are two listed on our map. Jason thinks it is the closer one, but he's not sure. The roads are curvy and narrow. Jason honks as we go around each bend in case a bus is coming. Buses do the same. Honking in India is polite. The sense you get from drivers is "honk honk, just coming round the bend."

We reach the first lookout. It's crowded with Indian families and vendors selling roasted corn and earmuffs. It is 60 degrees and the sun is shining. Jason pokes around and takes some photos. I sit on a bench and eat a cookie.

Jason returns. I am sort of sleeping. This is definitely not the right spot. He asks me if I want to try the next lookout, which is farther away, and he really isn't even sure it is the right one. "Of course we are trying," I say.

We drive on. The road gets smaller and the views get more spectacular. Steep hills are lined with manicured tea plantations. There are polka dots of workers hidden in the rows of bushes. The road is made of dirt now. We stop to let a goat cross.

There is a tower with large picture windows and a staircase that spirals around. I'm worried. The one from Jason's photo has no roof.

Beside the tower is a small path. I race down.

March 2001

January 2010

It's been repainted. Jason is glad it's not exactly the same. There is a steady flow of people climbing the steps. I march up to the top and find I need to rest before I can look over the edge.

To the left of the platform is a rocky area with more panoramic views and picnickers. The area is rimmed by a turquoise railing similar to the iron headboards found in brothels or little girls' rooms.

Bird's-eye view

I'm not hungry but Jason is. We stop at a restaurant just down the road. It's not fancy though it has the same views as the lookout. An Indian couple asks to join us. We welcome them.

It is a man and wife. They are both wearing polar fleece. She has earmuffs on. Her name is Chandra and his is Dilip. Chandra says, "It's freezing up here." Dilip adds, "Yes, it is freezing." I hear Chandra's teeth chattering. Jason tells them about the blizzard he saw in South Korea. Chandra and Dilip tell us they have been to Japan, South Africa, Paris, and Australia.

The waitress comes over. Everyone orders the veg meal but me. Chandra asks why I'm not eating, then quickly answers her own question correctly, I have a stomachache. She says she knows what will help, and barks some Hindi at the waitress.

Dilip owns a cement company. They have two children. Chandra's brother is studying business at Duke. Go Blue Devils.

Dilip and Chandra must be from an upper caste. They treat the people who run the restaurant badly. I'm embarrassed to be seated with them. If they acted this way in my father's restaurant they would be kicked out. Pronto.

Dilip asks about New York real estate. Jason and I have a rule about New York real estate: If it comes up, change the subject. We let the rule slide.

When the food arrives Chandra is explaining that the thing to do is buy lots of houses and rent them out. Chandra has ordered me idli to soothe my stomach. I eat them to be polite and soon my stomach feels better.

I have read about a tea factory that gives tours. It is on the way to Ooty. The drive back is long and full of curves that require honking.

We find the factory. I'm so excited to see how tea is made! Jason is excited too. He is about to shit himself.

Jason says the bathroom is disgusting. This makes sense. There are busloads of people here.

A guide gives an introduction in Hindi. He uses a laser pointer and a large sign to explain the steps of making tea. Then he sets us off on a walking path through the factory.

No surprising techniques or tools. The last stop of the tour is a free sample of the tea. There is a mountain of used cups next to a half-full garbage can with a sad sign.

Trash can plea

We need to return the motorcycle before the ten-year-old's bedtime. It's making a funny noise but manages to hold out.

I want to go sleep in our cottage, but Jason and I have another stupid rule: Push it. I say we should go to the thread garden. Jason is game.

I read about the thread garden in a guidebook. The review declared it a sad waste of time.

We take a rickshaw to the garden. Ooty is not as posh as I thought. I can see lush hills past the short concrete buildings, but what I smell is burning garbage.

FIRST TIME IN THE WORLD

The ticket seller tells us the garden took fifty women twenty years to complete. It is a room the size of an eighteen-wheeler truck. There are plants and flowers made of only thread. I want to like it but don't. It just seems like a waste of fifty women's patience. Jason doesn't like it either. He takes a few photos because we paid extra for a camera pass.

Not like we wanted to.

I bring up my desire to nap, but Jason thinks we should check out the lake and amusement park across the street.

The amusement park's main draw seems to be bumper cars and a mechanical bull. The lake has a boathouse that rents paddle boats shaped like giant swans and ducks. There are pony rides and cotton candy. Jason and I stick out here. On top of being the only foreigners, we are the only people with no children. Further on is a garden and a walking trail. Jason wants to keep exploring. I veto. I'm done pushing it.

I send short e-mails to my family using the messed-up keyboard. I make sure not to mention the vomiting.

We eat dinner at our hotel in the wood-paneled room from another era. A man is playing live piano. They are children's songs. "Mary Had a Little Lamb," "Polly-Wolly-Doodle," "Frère Jacques." Jason's face is lit by candlelight.

One of my mom's favorite restaurants was in the Mexico Pavilion at Epcot. It's the only restaurant our family ever went where we needed reservations. The place had Mayan ruins and was modeled after a seventeenth-century hacienda. Donald Duck would walk through the tables wearing a sombrero. Walt Disney copied the world so well that sometimes when Jason and I travel, real life seems fake.

9.

Redo breakfast. Manage to keep it all down. We pack up and say good-bye to my convalescing cottage.

The monkeys don't seem as sneaky going down the mountain. We are riding in an old white taxi called an Ambassador. There is no A/C but it's charming. Our driver doesn't speak English. The trip to Mysore is three hours. Jason puts his head in my lap and takes a nap.

The driver drops us off at our hotel. The innkeeper opens a big ledger book and enters Jason's good name. Our room is huge. It feels like a storage unit. I refill my tote bag with snacks from my reserve of cookies and juice boxes. Jason organizes his shot and unshot film.

Before we left home, I cut our guidebooks into sections and added computer printouts. Jason then spiral-bound each region with a generic cardboard cover. This makes our guidebooks inconspicuous and lightweight. I pick out a place across town for lunch that I think Jason will like.

Mysore is a largish city. The sidewalks are uneven. I lag behind a little, trying to make sure I don't stumble. I'm sweating in my new-wave shalwar kameez. We see some cows finding shade in a gas station that look like a *Far Side* cartoon come to life. Jason takes my hand because I am walking too slowly.

The lunch place is packed. We wait on line. A young boy clears our table and sets down banana leaves to act as plates. We get the veg meal like everyone else. There are lots of very young boys working here, clearing and setting tables. The boys can't be more than eight years old. I worked as a kid doing these same tasks at my family's restaurant, but it wasn't the same.

Despite getting to use a leaf as a plate, I eat only the rice. Jason gets seconds and is a pig in shit happy.

We go to the central market. There are pyramids of oranges and skate ramps of carrots. Every one has battered scoops and scales. All the stalls seem to be run by families. I love it here.

Star of Mysore

Noon

Chamundi Hill overlooks Mysore. At the top is a temple that Jason wants to see. We hail a rickshaw. The driver won't tell us the price till we start to walk away, and then it is too high. We grab another, more reasonable rickshaw.

The road spirals up the hill. At the summit we walk past men trying to sell soft drinks and trinkets. The salesmen say, "Hello, my friends" as we pass. One greets us with *"Bonjour, mes amis"* and another *"Ciao, amici."*

A monk has just closed the temple doors. He tells us it will open again in an hour and a half.

We walk to the edge of the hill. Mysore spreads below and off in the distance are the Nilgiri mountains we have just left. Jason and I split an orange. A young man approaches us and says, "Do you have American quarter for my collection? United States capital: Washington, D.C. United States president: Barack Obama." We ignore him.

There are monkeys climbing all over the temple using its sculptures and carvings as footholds.

Monkey House

A line has formed to get in the temple, which opens in forty-five minutes. Everyone is barefoot. No shoes allowed. I take mine off and put them in my bag. The stone street is still warm from the sun. A guy walks by the line selling postcards of the temple. Jason buys some.

The line is starting to move. "I'm not going in. I'm scared. I'll meet you at the exit," I say to Jason. He tells me I have to go in, that he wants me to. Then he cinches it with "I dare you."

The "If you dare me, I will do it" law. My third date with Jason involved picking up contact sheets at his photo lab. The place is out of business now. A sweet guy named Ray worked there. Like everyone, Ray treated Jason special. He invited us into his office.

They talked about Kodak Portra paper and billing. Ray faced away to get something. Jason whispered "I dare you to touch the back of Ray's neck."

Ray whipped around after I did it. Jason and I tensed up, ready to be punished, but Ray wasn't pissed. He was even friendlier than before. Suddenly we were talking about things unrelated to photography. The back of Ray's neck was like King Hippo's belly button, that weak spot in the video game that lets the guard down.

We go through a metal detector that Jason's camera and belt buckle don't set off. Now we are inside the temple, which is crammed full of people.

We are moving in mass toward the center of the temple. I'm still afraid. We reach the sanctum and there is an open silver door to a room. As I am pushed past it I get a glimpse. Inside there are monks serving a gold statue. The crowd pushes me out into a courtyard where people are praying and making offerings. Several people have brought coconuts and break them.

I can't relate to this frenzy. Religion didn't exist in my family. My mother and father were Jews from the Bronx, but this is the first temple I've ever been to.

Say "Om"

10.

There is no hot water or breakfast at our hotel. I don't mind. The place has a low-key character that is winning.

I've read about two factories that give tours. One makes silk and the other sandalwood oil.

At the silk factory, we check our bags with the guard and are allowed to wander the campus unattended. I was hoping there would be silkworms feeding on mulberry leaves, but the factory buys raw silk in bulk. It has been running since 1930 and looks like nothing has changed.

The place is going full speed. A worker comes up to us, he shakes our hand. It is hard to understand him. His English is perfect but the noise from the machines drowns him out.

The driver has trouble finding the second factory. I have an epiphany that there are more roads named after Gandhi than Martin Luther King.

The factory is deserted except for a guard and a tour guide. Sandalwood has become endangered in India. So it is a tour of an ex-sandalwood factory. The tour is short. At the end, the guide tries to sell us incense.

The streets are lined with small shops. Most places you go into have a large photo of the ancestor who started the business, hanging on the wall. I see a computer store. Jason has no idea why I want to go in.

The man behind the counter is wearing a suit and speaks English. I ask him for a USB keyboard. He shows us two and we buy the nicer one. Small talk turns to politics. The man is soft-spoken like Jason and they hit it off. As we are leaving, the man gives Jason his business card and says, "If you find yourself in any trouble, please call on me, and I will try to help." I read this two ways: 1. Wow, that is so sweet. 2. What kind of fucking trouble is he talking about?

There is a fantastic black-and-white photo of Jason taken from his first trip. He's wearing a lungi standing next to a vase of roses with a little mustache drawn on him. He got the photo done at a portrait studio in Madurai. He wants to get one done of us, together. Badly.

All the portrait studios we see have gone digital. We keep searching and find a little studio that looks promising. No one is there but the doors are propped open. We sit down and wait.

For display only

After forty minutes the shopkeeper returns. He is drunk. This does not stop Jason from asking him to take our photo with the caveat that he use film. The drunk tells us that it is not possible. The problem is, the photochemicals he needs are no longer sold in Mysore. Now he only mats and frames photos. We accept defeat.

The street smells like ink. Small shops are busting with paper and presses. Jason spots a stall with old wooden drawers. They are not mounted on the wall to display tchotchkes, but hold metal type as they were meant to. It is a working letterpress shop. We circle the block and powwow as to what we should make.

The answer is pads of paper with friends' nicknames printed on them. The printer's hair is black with silver sideburns, his name is Harry with an *i*.

Hari explains the metal type is only for making rubber stamps. Nobody uses movable type anymore, maybe one shop, but they use Hindi characters, not English. We are bummed. It passes. Hari can have the pads made with offset printing by the day after tomorrow. This sounds good. Hari starts up his computer and opens the program Adobe PageMaker 2.0. He lays out a document and shows us all the fonts he has. **Story Book** is highly recommended. I'm game for the font. It feels vaguely Indian. Jason vetoes. We have a friend nicknamed Wizard. Jason points out **Wizard** in Story Book looks like a bad graphic design student exercise. Akin to writing the word "S L O W" with extra kerning. We go for the safe choice. A bootleg version of the font: **SPARTAN**.

We don't want a border but are told we need one. The paper cutters won't know where to cut and the names will not be centered. We trust Hari on this and put a double-lined border around the pad. We choose a soft pulpy paper in pink, blue, and green. Jason puts down a deposit and shakes Hari's hand.

Oxen with painted horns pull carts. Every once in a while a few goats pass us. Jason says to watch where I walk. Dog shit on sneakers is one thing, but oxen shit in sandals is another.

Our hotel was built a long time ago with architecture that was created for this climate. I sit on the cool marble floor and open the keyboard box with cheesy stock photos that remind me of home. It takes me barely a minute to get it working. Jason is happy. This makes me happy.

11.

The ticket reservation office is crowded. I take a number and think about how India's trains are overbooked and America's trains are underbooked.

Our number is called. Jason goes to the counter and tries to buy us tickets on the Mysore express that leaves tomorrow night.

It is fully reserved. We need to get a special exception ticket.

Papers are stacked high next to rotary telephones and racks of rubber stamps. Images of a recent solar eclipse are displayed on a computer monitor. A man with a pocket protector helps us. Jason fills out some forms and pays the fare. The ticket has no seat numbers. We need to check the side of the train. If our names are listed, we have seats, if not we can get a refund. I'm worried this will ruin our plan. Jason isn't.

We walk toward the market to buy more oranges.

Switchplates

Museum of Mankind

Tidy whities

Coming soon

I keep almost losing my balance. It may be because of my flimsy shoes or the erratic sidewalks, I'm not sure. There is a fancy chain called Café Coffee Day that is similar to Starbucks. We go there to escape the heat and get real coffee. They are playing Bryan Adams on a loop. We split a pack of honey oatmeal cookies and write some postcards.

In the evening, crowds of people file into a public auditorium. We follow them. Rows of seats lead to a stage with Moorish details. Large industrial fans jut out of pillars that line the wall. A pack of eight-year-olds dressed like sultans complete with fake beards is running wild. It's a school talent show. We grab some seats. The woman sitting in front of us has white flowers braided in her hair. The show is about to start. Fathers arrive at the last minute.

The lights dim and the curtain opens. Teachers sit on red cushioned chairs behind a banquet table. The ceremony is held in a mix of Hindi and English and conducted by two teenage girls with thick accents. They take turns at the microphone. One by one, floral garlands are placed around the teachers' necks. The teachers are given gifts and thanks. The curtain closes. There is a long pause.

"I hope you all enjoy the rhythmic movements of these little ones," the two girls announce in unison. The curtains open. The table has been replaced by a dozen three-year-olds. The little girls are wearing lots of makeup and the boys tuxedos. "We Like to Party" by the Vengaboys comes blaring out of the speakers. One child wanders offstage, only to be caught and brought back.

The next acts are mostly babies dancing to Jock Jams. The music is impossibly loud. Finally, an act comes on that is set to Indian music. Six-year-old boys and girls are paired up. They walk hand in hand down an imaginary catwalk. It is a fashion show of Indian wedding dresses through the history of time. The crowd explodes.

Talent show

12.

Hari is washing his stall with a pail of soapy water and a sponge. His small daughter helps. We wait till they finish.

The pads are ready. They are perfect.

This post office is a mess. There are packages strewn about. It is as if we are shoving the pads into a bottle and throwing them into the ocean.

There is a folk museum on the Mysore University campus I want to see. Jason hails us a rickshaw. The driver uses the meter! We have gotten the only honest driver in Mysore.

The campus is well cared for. It is much cleaner here than in the city. We ask a student where the museum is. It is at another campus down the road. By the time we reach the museum, they are just closing for lunch. They will open in an hour and a half.

Mysore University

The first room has glass display cases full of everyday objects that belonged to famous Indian authors. I've never heard of any of these writers. A guard tells us the electricity in the rest of the museum is broken.

We can see most of the exhibits because the building has windows and skylights everywhere. I see rooms full of utensils, puppets, costumes, tools, and more. Some of the displays are made by simply laying the items out on the floor or leaning them up against a wall.

I come to a pitch-black room with household equipment. There is a silhouette of what looks to be an old scientific scale but on closer inspection it's a typewriter made for extra-wide documents. If we had another day, I would buy a flashlight and come back.

A large dot-matrix printout is taped to the side of the train. Our names are listed next to seat numbers. Our special exception has come through.

The train has baby-blue interior. There is a businessman sitting across from us. We get to talking. He lives in Chennai and his name is Upen. He's heading home after buying a coffee farm in the Nilgiri Mountains for his boss. His company has an office in Wisconsin. Upen, like almost 40% of Indians, is vegetarian. He tells us funny stories about trying to eat in Wisconsin that always end up with him at Pizza Hut. Something Upen wants America to know is that eggs are not vegetarian.

Jason asks him for a suggestion of a good place to eat in Chennai. Upen answers immediately: "Annalakshmi. It is expensive but all the profits go to charity and it is the best vegetarian restaurant in the world." Upen is shocked that we plan on spending two days in Chennai as tourists. He tells us we should go to Mamallapuram instead.

13.

Chennai central, rickshaw drivers hound us. A driver starts pulling at Jason's bag. Jason pushes him off and nearly gets in a fight. We walk for a block or two and hail a rickshaw that's not so rabid.

The air is heavy with exhaust. Honking is incessant, and not polite. We weave in and out of buses that are so crowded people are hanging off. I feel tired and nauseous. It is filthy here and not in a natural way, more in a trash and piss on the street way.

The front desk clerk is wearing an aqua sari with gold trim. She tells us they are fully booked and our reservation is not valid.

Jason figures the hotel had enough walk-ins and bumped us to avoid paying our booking agent. The lady in the aqua sari will not let us use the hotel's telephone even to call a toll-free number. I stay with the bags while Jason finds a phone booth.

He is gone a long time. I get scared. I set a twenty-minute timer on my phone. If the timer goes off I will do something. I am down to six minutes. Jason pops his head in the lobby. The problem isn't solved yet, he is just checking in. I reset my timer to an hour.

Jason returns. All the accommodations listed in our spiral-bound book are full. The booking agent managed to get us a reservation at an apartment-hotel across town. Jason wrangles another rickshaw and we set off. Driving here is fucking terrifying. Streets are two-way with no lane separation.

The apartment-hotel is depressing. The only window is covered by an iron gate and faces a wall. I'm just happy there is a Western-style toilet. I've had to go since the train station.

It is excruciating. Every time I try to push, my head explodes. Migraines happen worst when I'm stressed. And though he's here with me now, I am still scared at the thought of Jason not coming back from the phone booth.

My mother would swoop in when I had a headache. She'd turn off the lights and give me a rose quartz crystal to rub. I was told to chant "I will be well." When I told her it wasn't working, she would give me an amethyst.

"Chennai is a nightmare," Jason says as I come out of the bathroom. He is stressed too. I squeeze his shoulders and pull down till my hand gets snagged at the wrist. It looks like I'm trying to milk his arms. When we were dating, Jason did this to me. It was one of the first times he touched me. He asked me after, "Doesn't it feel good?" I told him I thought it was weird and, in fact, didn't really feel good. Now whenever Jason is down, I rub his arms like this.

We decide to take Upen's advice on Mamallapuram. It is a UNESCO World Heritage site and only an hour away. Jason visited there on his last trip but says I will like it and should see it.

At home I like to carry my own bags. Room service strikes me as antisocial and lukewarm. Not here. Not today. Jason finds me a deluxe hotel just outside Mamallapuram. He books the best room they have for tomorrow night. We are excited about the complimentary bicycles.

Walking here is unpleasant and dangerous. Jason says Chennai didn't use to be this way. He is shocked that this is the same city he was in ten years ago. There were not so many cars. He rode a motorcycle and saw live music at night. The venues were half empty and dark. He sat on cushions next to old people falling asleep.

The car hire office is hard to find. There are low drop ceilings above gray desks with piles of paper. Jason crouches so he doesn't bump his head. A car will pick us up in the morning. A chubby man fills out a form and takes our deposit. He makes a quick phone call in Hindi.

A panel of the drop ceiling lifts up and an arm reaches down with a hand held out.

Our form is placed in the hand, which is then pulled up and the ceiling panel is put back in place. "We save on rent this way," the chubby man says.

People on the way to a wedding have decorated their car with packing tape and roses. Near the car we see a sign for an Internet and STDs. *STD* means long-distance calling in India.

There are eight computers, but seven are in use. Jason goes first.

An architecture magazine has e-mailed Jason with a job. He needs to fly to Las Vegas when we get home. Jason and I work freelance. He is a photographer and I am an illustrator. We are lucky jobs often seem to fall in sync with our travels.

I read an e-mail from my sister. She is ratting out my dad. He has put a whole section of coconut drinks on the menu to go along with the photo of me. I receive an e-mail about a job too. It's the cover of the *New York Times Book Review*. The illustration is due a week after we get home. I print out the article for two cents a page.

We make our way to a Café Coffee Day and split a pack of honey oat cookies. Jason writes postcards. I read the book review twice and scribble on the margins. My job is to create a visual that helps or hooks the reader. I've been an illustrator for five years. I now call illustrations "illos" and the art director "A.D."

The A.D. is a cutman, phone-a-friend, and goalie. A.D.s don't tell an illustrator what to draw, they explain the needs of the layout and editors. Finding what to draw is like a game, complete with countdown clocks and wah-wah sounds.

Every illo has different rules. Covers are harder than inside illos. They need to read quicker, be larger, and withstand more scrutiny. My cover strategy is keep it simple.

Funny Bone Anatomist

A transversal cut through wit, not for laughs but to examine its mechanisms.

BY WILLIAM GRIMES

WE know that Yorick was a fellow of infinite jest. But what exactly was his boffo material? Did he slay them with borscht-belt one-liners, or did he stick to observational humor — Seinfeld-like riffs on the miseries of Danish weather? Alas, we cannot know. But it seems fairly certain that even melancholy Danes prized a choice punch line, like the Romans and the Greeks before them.

In "Stop Me if You've Heard This," his wispy inquiry into the history and philosophy of jokes,

---

STOP ME IF YOU'VE HEARD THIS
A History and Philosophy of Jokes.
By Jim Holt.
141 pp. W. W. Norton & Company.
$15.95.

Jim Holt offers up a choice one from ancient times. Talkative barber to customer: "How shall I cut your hair?" Customer: "In silence."

Bada-bing.

This knee-slapper comes from "Philogelos," or "Laughter-Lover,"

Beatrice bristles at Benedick's accusation that her "good wit" comes straight from "The Hundred Merry Tales." It's a joke book, just like the Georgian classic "Joe Miller's Jests," a collection so popular that before long any stale joke was dismissed as "a Joe Miller."

Holt devotes loving attention to one of his modern-day heroes, Gershon Legman, the compiler of an obsessively annotated 1968 smut fest with the alluring title "Rationale of the Dirty Joke." Legman, an associate of Alfred Kinsey's, was the author of "Oragenitalism" (subtitled "An Encyclopaedic Outline of Oral Tech-

cal survey makes clear, jokes present a quickly moving target. Certain themes seem to be eternal, but others are not. Lettuce, probably because of its association with sexual potency (and its opposite), struck the Romans as hilarious. Larry the Cable Guy would probably have bombed in the Colosseum.

The packaging changes too. Henny Youngman could have used the Greek barber joke, but would the quick-witted Beatrice have understood the meta-humor of Steven Wright, whose nonjokes rely on the audience's recognition that the standard joke format has been turned inside out?

The New York Times Book Review (inside)
Stop Me If You've Heard This: A History and Philosophy of Jokes
by Jim Holt

The New York Times Book Review (cover)
The Wilderness Warrior: Theodore Roosevelt and the Crusade for America
by Douglas Brinkley

It's dinnertime. Annalakshmi seems to be run by a very gentle cult. There are wood carvings and decoration on every surface. The whole place has an orange hue. It's very Zen, especially in contrast to what lies outside.

The food comes on silver plates. Our meal takes two hours, though it doesn't feel like it. No question, it is the best meal we've had in India. Jason makes me check out the bathroom before we leave because he says it looks like a dungeon.

It totally looks like a dungeon.

We walk toward a pack of rickshaws. As I approach, I see it is a crowd of people living in the street. Some of them are rickshaw drivers. The rickshaws are not for hire. Thin families are asleep, illuminated by bright streetlamps. Men share lentils around a makeshift table. The smells make me nauseous and the traffic is so loud my ears ring. I bury my face in my shalwar kameez. Jason spots an on-duty rickshaw across the road.

14.

A guard from Third Eye Security is protecting the entrance to our apartment-hotel. We drink juice boxes and eat cookies for breakfast while sitting on our bags. Our car arrives. The driver is friendly and speaks English.

The road to Mamallapuram is much better maintained than other roads we've been on. Jason gazes out the window. I lean on him and try to think of an idea for the book review job. I hit on an idea that works but still need to think of a back-pocket idea. I become tired and put my pencil down.

There is a sign for a crocodile farm. I have seen this sign in Jason's contact sheets from his first trip to India. We are getting close.

A woman in a sari places a floral garland around my neck and gives me a tall glass of fresh pomegranate juice.

We are early; our cottage is still being cleaned and prepared. Jason encourages me to check out the beach, while he does the paperwork.

I walk down a path past a cage of parrots and an L-shaped pool. There is a small private beach. I take off my shoes and lie in a hammock. I can see the ocean between my toes. I've never stayed at a place like this. I never wanted to before.

Jason finds me in my shalwar kameez, a lei around my neck, beside a palm tree and a hut. The bikes and our room are ready whenever we want. Also, he has scored the mother lode of postcards at the hotel gift shop.

It's called the wooden cottage and is aptly named. It is just how I imagine a luxury suite on the *Titanic* looked.

We will work now and ride bikes to Mamallapuram after lunch, when the sun is less harsh. I sit in bed with hotel stationery and draw a sketch of my idea for the book review illo. I want to brainstorm, but close my eyes instead.

Jason wakes me up. He is ordering lunch. While I was asleep he has finished and sent off the photo-blog interview.

Fresh-cut orchids decorate the table. My food tastes funny but I ignore it and chow down.

It feels good to be on a bicycle, but I lag behind. My handlebars are a bit wonky, which makes it hard to ride straight. We are hugging the side of the highway. It is three miles to Mamallapuram.

Signs advertise Internet, ATMs, and STDs. We ride past backpackers and tour buses. Jason leads us to the Pancha Rathas. The admission price is eight times higher if you are not Indian. There must have been problems with forgeries because the tickets are printed in full color with a hologram.

Inside the gate people pet and climb half-carved seventh-century rocks. I sit in a tree-house-size stone temple and rest.

Pancha Rathas

"Hello, ladies"

We go to a park that is filled with hills, trees, and sculpted rocks. We are walking through a science-fiction movie. I fall in love with a crude carving that resembles corn on the cob. We come to a clearing with a giant bolder called Krishna's Butterball. It is poised to crush a group of Belgian teenagers sitting beneath it.

I watch while Jason climbs up to yet another temple carved in a giant rock. I wonder if I am so tired because I'm trying to process all the information I'm taking in. My brain feels like it is expanding too fast.

We ride our bikes down a historic street full of stone carvers who have been sculpting for generations. I have heard sound recordings made ten years ago of this very street. It does not sound the same. The "tink tink" has been replaced with "whir whir." Everyone is using electric grinders.

Jason takes photos of sculptures that our guidebook describes as tacky. I am sitting on an empty pedestal imitating a Hindu goddess, trying to make Jason laugh. A Japanese family passes me. They look very disappointed with this sculpture museum.

Call the doctor

It is good to be back in the *Titanic*. Jason tells me not to go to sleep.

Jason nudges me. He is hungry and thinks I should not be sleeping. We get room service again. It arrives accompanied by a bird of paradise in a crystal vase.

"Our buddy is back," Jason says. I tilt my head and Jason reaches under my chin.
"Got it?" I ask.
"Almost," Jason answers.

Technically our honeymoon was spent in Scranton, Pennsylvania. But a year later we went to France and rented a car. Every meal was a picnic and every day we attempted to speak French. I saw castles shrouded in fog, Louis Pasteur's soup, and a natural wonder called Chaos de la Balme.

Chaos de la Balme is French for deep woods filled with a crap-ton of monolithic boulders.

The trail was poorly marked, but the rocks were hard to miss. They were in giant formations with nicknames like Three Cheeses, Rock Goose, and Napoleon's Hat.

We came to a formation called River of Rocks. It was like a ball crawl, but with boulders. We turned into kids at Chuck E. Cheese's, jumping from rock to rock.

I stopped jumping. Jason asked why. I told him I was scared, that the gap was too big. He said it wasn't. I looked down. It wasn't bigger than any of the other spaces I had jumped across. "Can't do it," I said. "Sure you can. I dare you," Jason said.

Chapeau de Napoléon

It was twenty feet down. I hit the ground with a thud and blacked out. Jason jumped down immediately and woke me up. Then he scaled the giant boulders with me in tow. No idea how he found our way out of the woods or how he, all of a sudden, understood French.

I ended up with seven stitches under my chin. The doctor let me describe what happened in my pidgin French, though she spoke English.

It's all healed now, but one freak hair perpetually grows out of the scar. Every now and then Jason sweetly reaches under my chin and yanks the whisker out.

Jason's mutter paneer is gone. My plate is almost full. He tries to get me to eat more. I tell him I will, but after I lie down. I am tired.

Wild bird

Jason kisses my neck and wakes me gently. He wants to go for a walk on the beach.

Live music is spilling out of the hotel restaurant. A keyboardist and sitar player are jamming out the "Axel F" theme from *Beverly Hills Cop*. We watch them through the lattice walls that form the dining area.

It is very dark. All the hammocks have been taken down. Lying on the sand, we talk about how far ocean currents can travel. I put my head on Jason's chest and drift out.

I wake up confused. Waves are crashing. A group is laughing at a man laying in the sand. Another man falls down and the laughing gets louder. They are all hammered.

Jason guides me back to the cottage. I stumble to the bathroom in time to puke out dinner and lunch.

Postcard

15.

Breakfast waits under silver domes and comes with a newspaper. Jason has ordered us idli and coffee with sugar on the side. I am feeling better and e-mail my book review sketch to the art director although I don't have a backup plan yet.

The Fall plays on a loop from Jason's computer. We cut up the newspaper and make postcard collages to send to friends. Jason asks if I want to spend the rest of the day here rather than Chennai.

I don't want to stay. This place makes me feel weird. The exclusivity grosses me out. No idea why I wanted a luxury hotel so bad. Normally I beg Jason to stay at hotels with paper bath mats and a view of our car.

I'm afraid, deep down, I am not who I think I am, but chalk it up to a stomachache and tell Jason it is time to go.

Almost there

As soon as we get near Chennai the traffic starts. Rickshaws and motorcycles wedge between buses and cars like grout. The air is thick. We roll up all the windows.

Third Eye is still on duty. An Indian family sits on the black pleather sofa in the communal room. I eat some cookies and tell Jason that I actually like this apartment-hotel. He says it is growing on him too.

We stop in a market and emerge an hour later with a pack of white undershirts and my snack bag refilled.

Every weekend my family went to a supermarket in New Jersey. While my parents shopped for the restaurant, we kids were free to roam the aisles. Charlie would poke holes in the vacuum-packed coffee. Danny flew around in his favorite pajamas. Zack crawled the linoleum wearing shirts that had *Charlie* handpainted on them.

Once an announcement came over the PA: "Will the parents of the lost boy with the cape please report to the courtesy counter."

My mom went to see what was up.

A stock girl had found Danny climbing toward the green spaghetti. She asked who he was. "Superman!" Danny answered.

"Who are you really?" the stock girl asked. Danny motioned for her to come close. She leaned down and he whispered "Clark Kent."

16.

We are flying on Kingfisher Airlines. The airline is named after a beer that was named after a bird. I tell Jason they are lucky their beer wasn't called Rolling Rock. Jason says he would fly Southern Comfort.

The bus that is taking us to the plane has had all the factory-issued seats ripped out. They have been replaced with giant lipstick-red sofas and lounge chairs. The bus can now hold less than half the people it was meant to.

A stewardess welcomes us aboard. The airplane is spotless and brand new. It makes no difference which side of the bed we sleep on, but Jason always gets the aisle seat and I the window.

Reentry

The buildings have more character than before. Traffic is civilized compared to Chennai. The dirt and piss on the streets is more of a patina than a blight. Mumbai reminds me of how wild New York felt when I was a kid. I like it.

The blue-striped awning of our original hotel welcomes us back. Jason requests the same room we stayed in before. I lie down on the bed. The thin blanket and sheets are pulled comically tight.

It's Sunday. The parks are full of people playing cricket. A group of young boys asks Jason to take their photos. Jason says no and walks away.

Sunday matches

The tickets have seat numbers. An usher leads us to our row. A small group of Indians in polo shirts are seated across the aisle. There are about two hundred empty seats in front of us. The lights dim and the group of Indians stands up. Slow-motion footage of a waving Indian flag is projected. Jason and I stand too. The Indian national anthem is sung by two elderly women. The footage cuts back and forth between them and the waving flag. The voices are weathered and emotional. It is quite beautiful. It is a hard act to follow. Especially if you are an American movie based on a children's book.

The film stars a little boy who is dealing with anger. His snow fort gets smashed, he bites his mom. The tantrums seem so stupid here. Maybe it would resonate if his mother forced him to work in a carpet factory.

It's a shock to leave the dark cool theater and hit the hot crowded streets. We cut through a park. People are still playing cricket.

At a café we order some tea. It's just boiled ginger with honey but it's tasty. I write it down in my notebook so I can remember to make it at home. We sip it slowly. I tell Jason I am spoiled and take things for granted. He says he does too. I think about Einstein's theory of special relativity and wonder if he ever went to India.

There are so many people. Mumbai has so many people. Vendors sell fresh sugarcane juice and electric tennis racquets that zap bugs. Jason buys a bag to carry the goods we bought home. He haggles and gets four cents knocked off the price.

We pass a flickering flame. It is roasting mini peanuts. Jason points at the nuts and signals two. The vendor scoops some into paper cones. Peanuts taste better hot and from a paper cone.

17.

A bellboy gives us a claim tag for our luggage.

The Dr. Bhau Daji Lad Museum (aka City Museum) is the oldest museum in Mumbai. The first hall is titled "Industrial Arts." There are objects from all over India. Each one sits next to a clay diorama that shows how and where it was made. It is like visiting a hundred factories!

Upstairs, small clay figures depict hundreds of occupations and religions. They give a sense of everyday life in nineteenth-century Mumbai. There is a peanut seller in one of the cases. His paper cones are the size of sesame seeds.

Behind the City Museum is a zoo. But people are using it more as a park. It is overgrown and falling apart. There are not very many animals. Though there is a badass rhinoceros.

Old sign

We take a taxi to an Internet café. The art director for the book review likes my idea but couldn't get it by his editor. I write him that I will think of a new one. Jason has a lot of e-mails to deal with. I take the opportunity to brainstorm.

After twenty minutes I scrunch my face and rest my forehead in my palms. I've given myself a headache and have no ideas to show for it. Jason points out a sign above us:

I think of Johnny Appleseed wearing a cooking pot for a hat. When I was six, I wrote a story about him. I finished the book with "The And." I was treated like a prodigy.

My dad would show the last page of the book to friends and strangers. He'd say it was wiser and more elegant than anything he'd ever read. That there is no end to any story. One never has a full awareness of death. And even when you do die the earth goes on, the children have children. Space certainly doesn't have an end, only an "and."

Airport security. Boys on the left. Girls on the right. I tell Jason I will race him. The woman in front of me has an infant. The guards are thorough. They make her taste the milk from the baby's bottle before they will allow it through. Indian women wear a lot of jewelry and they forget to take it off. This gives the boys an advantage.

Jason is afraid the X-ray machines will mess up his film. He tries to get it hand-checked. They won't do it. Security finds his camera and request for a hand check suspicious and pulls him aside. No contest. I win.

The flight is full and smells like curry. Sixteen hours till New York.

Double duty

18.

The air is clean and weightless. Our breathing sounds like a perverted prank call. We are at JFK. Travelers pay three dollars to rent carts for five minutes. Planes circle overhead. The roads are all paved.

We drive toward home and pass what is left of the 1964 World's Fair. Snow dusts the Arctic on the Unisphere. The stainless steel earth was made to represent "Man's Achievement on a Shrinking Globe in an Expanding Universe." But it's now just a symbol of Queens.

The apartment is as we left it. A small room with a bed and two desks. On the wall is a sign I bought at a shoe repair shop on the Lower East Side. After the man agreed to sell it to me he went to the back of his store and returned with a handful of dead batteries. He poured them into my hands and said "in case any fall off."

Our luggage takes up half the apartment. I drink tap water while Jason starts up his computer. It is 8 a.m. The smell of bacon is wafting up from my favorite deli below.

Downstairs I am greeted with "Two eggs, toasted bialy." I nod yes to my nickname. On the wall is a framed clipping from a newspaper. The story is about a dangerous intersection located in downtown Brooklyn. The article has a photo of some blurry cars and my deli's awning circled proudly in red marker.

In the photo, "You go girl" is spray-painted above my deli. I always took the turquoise bubble letters to heart and was sad last year when my landlord painted over the graffiti.

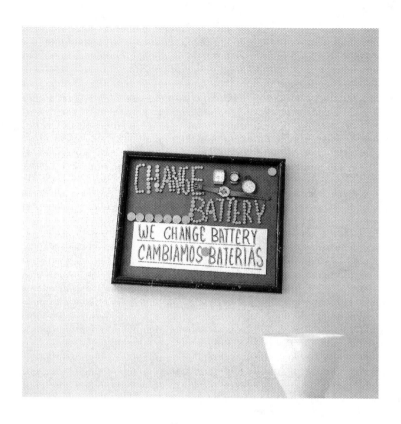

Back home

We listen to public radio. Jason clears his desk because we have no other place to eat. There was a terrible earthquake in Chile. A Jimi Hendrix video game is in development. The first Superman comic has sold at auction for one million dollars. Our bialys are gone.

Jason gathers his things. He is taking his laptop to a computer repair shop in Manhattan. One of my first jobs was repairing laser printers there. It was a good place to work. They had a porch swing and an old Coke machine. Free lunch on Wednesdays and health care.

My favorite problem to fix was if the pages of a laserwriter had ghosting. I'd have to take apart the whole printer, vacuuming all the nooks and crannies, until I got to the heart, which was a black plastic case marked with lightning bolts and caution signs.

Ignoring the warnings, I'd unscrew the cover to get to the optics.

They would be decorated with dust in the same exact pattern as the ghosting on the page. After wiping and polishing them, I'd close the case back up. Then remove a fan caked in dust and replace it with a brand-new one that had better blades. I'd put the whole thing back together, and print a hundred pages to prove the machine was fixed.

I'm about to fall asleep and surrender to jet lag. Jason tells me I should try to get some sun. I take this as a dare to be less jet-lagged than him.

Jury rig

My bike has been on the street alone for two weeks. The bike's basket is full of garbage. Candy wrappers and soda cans rattle as I make my way to Manhattan. I pull up next to a trash can and try to throw away the debris from my basket without dismounting. I nearly topple over.

Riding over the Brooklyn Bridge, people smile at me but don't move out of the way. They are posing for a picture.

The cap to my bell was stolen. It no longer has a reason to exist. I part the crowds by chanting "Bicycle, bicycle, bicycle," as if I am selling a frozen treat on a stick. The bike veers left and almost takes out a Chinese couple. I apologize and continue on like a pilot with engine failure.

The owner of the bike shop has black fingernails. He isn't Goth. It's grease. He is more likely a skinhead, though his head is not shaved. He wears tight acid-washed jeans with tiny red suspenders. Hard-core music blares from the back. I don't think he is a neo-Nazi. This is confirmed by the sticker of Bob Marley on the cash register.

This shop sells only old bikes. I can't bring my bike to a new bike store. It is not that kind of bike. The owner diagnoses the problem as unaligned wheels. I am lucky he can fix it right now.

I wait on a bench outside next to the complimentary air hose. In front of me are some dirty bikes being washed slowly by a man who smells like whiskey. He is wearing layers of clothes making him resemble a gobstopper.

The owner has finished fixing my bike. He wheels it out and sets it in front of me. As soon as the owner's back is turned, the gobstopper gives him the finger with both hands.

Brownian motion transports me uptown. The bike is in no visible way fixed. I dismount and roll it alongside me.

The Morgan Library has recently been renovated. A modern glass piazza has been poetically wedged between two historic buildings. The ticket and coat check staff are better dressed than me. Classical music plays faintly.

Below the main level I make a pit stop. The restroom is spotless and the toilet paper plentiful. Brass water fountains sparkle.

A diorama of the library and its new glass piazza are on display. The model is built from delicate blond wood. The miniature Morgan shrinks further as a glass elevator lifts me to the exhibition space. My book review job is about a chick-lit blockbuster. I have come here hoping that "A Woman's Wit: Jane Austen's Life and Legacy" will shake an idea loose.

A Modern Belle going to the Rooms at Bath.

James Gillray cartoon

Color prints of James Gillray cartoons are mixed in with Austen's letters.

The exhibit description states that Austen was inspired by satirical cartoons. The selected prints are amusing caricatures that make it easy to see the connection to Austen's writings.

I learn paper was so valuable that most of her letters were cross-written and don't have a square centimeter of blank paper.

There is a sweet letter to her eight-year-old niece written backwards. It starts "I hsiw uoy a yppah wen raey" and is signed "Enaj Netsua."

My art director, Nicholas, calls. He has got a copy of the chick-lit blockbuster and wants to give it to me. His office is only five blocks away.

The *New York Times* has just moved to a brand-new glass sky-scraper. The old building had hot-metal presses in the basement, and a physical database with millions of photos and clippings known as "the morgue." Elevators in the new building don't have buttons. They magically know what floor you are going to.

Nicholas used to have his own office. Now he shares a giant cubicle in an open space filled with natural light. Everyone gets floor-to-ceiling windows.

I'm given the 304-page blockbuster. We talk about India and Jane Austen, while the blinds automatically adjust themselves as the sun gets higher.

It slips out that I have arrived this morning at 7:30 a.m. Nicholas once taught me how to make drawings "superblack" by adding a touch of yellow, magenta, and cyan. Now he sagely advises me to go home and rest.

As if we are in a children's book, my bike and I ride the subway together. We are tired and broken. I chain the bike to my usual pole with what appears to be a maximum security lock, but it's not. I got the lock for five euros in Amsterdam.

LoVE
U
LoT

Tucked between the screen and keyboard of my laptop is a note from Jason. An e-mail offers another job. It is a story for a Canadian magazine about a donut chain. The art director's name is Una.

Her name makes me think of Eugene O'Neill's daughter. By age seventeen, Oona O'Neill had dated J. D. Salinger, Orson Welles, and Charlie Chaplin. At age eighteen, she married Chaplin, who was fifty-four. After the wedding, Oona's father disowned her.

Oona and Chaplin had eight children. They were together until Chaplin died thirty-five years later. Eugene O'Neill never forgave Oona for marrying Chaplin and never saw her again.

I've seen a daughter of Oona and Charlie preform. The most graceful person I've ever seen. Her name is Victoria Chaplin. The show I saw her in was made of little moments. In one scene she wore a fancy dress that turned into a horse and galloped offstage.

There is a good amount of time till deadline and I like Una's name. I accept the job and ask her to send me the story.

One hundred pages into the book Nicholas has given me, I decide to stop reading and start working. I try to get up but can't. I am too wrapped up in the plot and my bedcovers.

At page 160, my phone rings. It is Jason asking to meet for Vietnamese in Chinatown. I haven't eaten since breakfast.

Jason has already gotten a table. In front of him sits a plate with one spring roll. The doily beneath it is stained with three greasy shadows. Jason tells me about the resort he will photograph in Vegas. The gambling retreat is made up of skyscrapers similar to Nicholas's new building. It has a "city" theme the same way Treasure Island Hotel and Casino has a "pirate" theme.

I am not sure how I have arrived home. Jason unlocks the door and heads upstairs. I follow but touch the top of each step, afraid to fall. Jason calls from above: "Beach Ball, you all right?"
"I'm okay," I answer. "Just struggling."

19.

In India, it is 3:30 in the afternoon. Here it is 6 a.m. Jason is awake too. I climb out of bed and am pulled to the ground. The floor is cold. Two squished sneakers and a tripod peek out from under the bedskirt. Jason asks from above if I'm okay. "The room is spinning," I answer. "Don't worry. You just got up too fast, that happens to me. Is it still happening?" Jason says.

It is dark outside, but traffic is already too loud to open the window. I make us coffee and am drawn back into the chick-lit blockbuster.

An hour later: Jason is showered and shaved, working at his desk in a button-down shirt and slacks. I resemble a person relaxing at the beach. Except the chick lit shades my eyes from the glow of Jason's computer rather than the sun. Competitive jet lag takes over. I get dressed and make us oatmeal with chopped almonds. The honey smells like fart. Jason says honey doesn't go bad and adds that archaeologists have found edible honey from the time of pharaohs. I put honey in his bowl and not mine.

We eat with our computers instead of each other. Una has e-mailed me the donut story. Thanks to my older brother Charlie, I watch a viral video of a carpenter. The man stands two yards from his targets in half-built homes. He shoots his tape measure out like a sniper. Lights turn off, radios on. He opens a Porta Potty door while someone is peeing. Each time his friends in Carhartt workwear cheer. Jason leans over my shoulder to watch.

I regularly illustrate a letters to the editor column for a craft magazine. They have sent me the story for their forthcoming issue.

A stranger wants to know when my novelty store will reopen. Rattlesnake eggs, paper umbrellas, arrow thru the head. I love novelties. In my spare time I make things that feed off this affection. Matchbooks, note cards, and more. I sell them in an online store. It's been closed while I was in India because I am the sole employee. I take down the closed message and make it so the website can accept orders again.

Washington Walnuts

I'm in the bathroom. There is a problem. It is painful. Well-meaning bonus sheets make life more difficult. The toilet paper holder was built into the wall when bonuses only came at Christmas. Jason has shoved the roll in as if it were a marshmallow. I wipe at the tears on my face with the three scraps of paper I manage to pull off.

Jason knocks. "You okay?" he asks. ". . . Migraine. Bad," I answer through the door.

I'm finally out of the bathroom. Jason leaves to have lunch with a friend. I take a break from the chick-lit job and work on the craft magazine story I have just received.

Q: Do you think of yourself as belonging to a crafts community?
A : Absolutely and it is international.

An idea is about to come to me. Another headache arrives instead. I decide to get some fresh air.

My family has run a restaurant most of my life. We have always called it The Store because before we ran a restaurant we ran a grocery store. Wood floors covered in sawdust and a screen door that slapped. Tin ceilings, powdered soap, gumball machines, cat food, and luncheon meat. My parents wore aprons over funny T-shirts and had pencils tucked behind their ears. Tuna fish cans and boxes of pasta were my building blocks.

It was a neighborhood place. Customers took care of the spawn while my parents took care of them.

At some point supermarket chains appeared and our rent was raised. In order to survive, the store became a restaurant. We never called it The Restaurant, though, always The Store.

My father is glad to see me. He hugs me and offers turkey hot from the oven. A joke about my surviving India is told as he sits down. He looks up at me after the punch line to see if I will laugh or scold him. I laugh.

Me

Zack shouts from the pickup window, "Welcome home. Don't make a fucking mess in my kitchen." Zack is my youngest brother. He is famous in our family for losing his virginity at thirteen and forgetting to put back my dad's pants after stealing cash while my father was asleep. Zack has changed. A lot.

"Your kitchen?" I say. "So you don't want me to cook this Saturday?" "No, I missed you, please work Saturday. Please. I have a bag of arugula in the walk-in," Zack replies.
"She goes right for the jugular. Just like that," my father says.

Today is Thursday. I cook brunch every Saturday. New Yorkers don't fuck around at brunch. Bacon, pancakes, maple syrup, butter, and unholy amounts of eggs. When Jason and I were courting, my egg-cracking prowess drove him nuts the way I imagine Marilyn Monroe's hips did Joe DiMaggio.

In under five minutes I make lunch. Zack starts to yell at me about the flour trail my ciabatta has left on the cutting board but is soon distracted by a check. I am unrepentant and glad not to be in his way.

There are a dozen customers. My father and brother know all of their names. I know half of them. My brother is making sliders, while my father holds court from his orthopedic chair.

I sit near my dad and eat my sandwich. I tell him about how there are more poor people in India, but they seem happier than the poor people here. My dad launches into a riff on the nature of being. When he is finished we return to topic. He concludes there is less of a stigma to being poor in India.

I gather some groceries to take home. Fresh turkey and a container of rice. A storage bag of arugula. Half a cucumber. Some walnuts. Zack and Dad call me a thief and let loose. It is good to be home.

In the subway station I start brainstorming on the craft illo again. Under the East River, I hit on it. I circle the drawing amid the nonworking doodles.

I'm finished. I wash off my pen nibs. If the idea still looks okay in the morning, I will e-mail it.

Waking up at 6 a.m. has its pros. It is barely 3 p.m. I try the book review illo again. Nothing.

Jason gets home. He is tired after eating pork with rice and beans at the restaurant where the waitress calls him Papi, but he lets me bounce ideas off him.

We can channel the way one another thinks. Jason flips the switch and turns my idea that doesn't work into one that does.

The sketch is Approved! Nicholas sends me layouts. The final illo is due tomorrow night.

I make dinner with the groceries I stole from The Store. A big salad of chopped turkey with walnuts and some rice on the side. We change Jason's desk into the dinner table. The salad tastes funny to me. I apologize several times. Jason says it tastes really good and that he loves this dinner. I am worried that I need to call my dad and tell him the turkey is funky, but I let it go.

Jason packs his luggage for Las Vegas while I draw the final art for the book review cover. I stop halfway through and decide to finish it in the morning. I am too tired to draw. It is still early in the evening. I lie down on the bed and read the Canadian donut story.

Jason is trying to take my shoes off. I hear them thud on the floor. He climbs into bed, and I fall back to sleep.

20.

Jason whispers good-bye as he heads for the airport. It is 6:30 a.m.

I've gotten out of bed too fast. The room is spinning. I ignore it and make coffee.

The craft magazine illo still looks alright. I e-mail it to the art director and move on to the book review.

My stomach is making funny noises. Is an older lady more likely to wear gold or silver jewelry? Photos of elderly women on the Internet suggest silver bracelets, but gold rings. Now I can finish coloring the illo.

I'm in front of the toilet. I've just vomited. My mouth tastes awful. A grid pattern is pressed into my knees. I crawl back to the bed, crying.

The alarm on my phone wakes me up. It's 9 a.m. I get dressed and go downstairs to my deli. I buy Fig Newtons and a can of ginger ale. My soda spills a little as I climb the stairs.

I pound Fig Newtons and finish the book review illo. Not my best. I want to start all over. As I think about this I start to get a headache. Oh fuck, the puking starts again.

Nicholas tells me the job is all set. Thank God.

My doctor works at a walk-in clinic. The waiting room is full of people that look sicker than me. I put my name on the list.

Dr. Williams is young and newly married with an adopted baby. He has taken his partner's last name. I congratulate him and call him by his new name even though it rhymes with "cock" and I still think of him as "Dr. Williams."

He asks me what is bothering me. I explain I was just in India, that I got ill there twice, that I woke up sick today, and that I really regret eating the lettuce in the airplane meal on the way home.

Dr. Williams wants to go to India, but with the new baby, doubts that will happen soon. He looks me over and asks questions about my symptoms.

My vitals look normal. There are a lot of things we can rule out. It could just be something I ate, but he isn't sure. A nurse takes my blood.

The best thing now is to rest. The blood results should be back next week. I tell him that I'm having migraine headaches again. I explain they are incredibly painful but are thankfully short.

Dr. Williams referred me to a neurologist I didn't like eight months ago named Dr. Schorr.

Williams wants me to see Schorr again. I ask him to recommend another neurologist. He can't. That's the only one he knows.

I call Dr. Schorr's office and I am given an appointment for next Friday.

It is bright outside. I am excited to enter my dim hallway despite its crooked stairs and strange odor. As soon as I set my things down, I am overcome. Nausea, vomiting, the whole nine. This is not jet lag.

I call my twin sister, Minda, at work. When she hears my voice, she asks me what's wrong.

Minda never gets sick. She looks the same as me, but her most prized possession is a hammer drill. She is at her office in TriBeCa arranging to film a raid in Florida with the U.S. drug czar. It is for the documentary she is producing that exposes the racial and financial biases of our drug laws. Late-night rides in squad cars, visiting prisons, and wearing bulletproof vests. My sister is a tank. A tank that hugs big and texts me five times a day to say she loves me.

She will pick me up in fifteen minutes. Can I make it downstairs? I tell her I can and shove my computer and some clothes in a backpack.

Minda

I wait, leaning on the wall that no longer tells me, "You go girl!" Minda waves to me from a taxi. I run across the street and hop in with her.

The last time Minda picked me up off a corner was after I got my wisdom teeth pulled. I was barefoot holding my shoes in one hand and waving at her with the other. I was grinning ear to ear, surprised and overjoyed to see her. I was high on laughing gas and anesthesia.

Before surgery the dentist asked, "Is the laughing gas working?" I asked back, "How do you know if it's working?" The dentist replied, "Do you feel different than you did five minutes ago?" I became hysterical and said, "I always feel different than five minutes ago."

Minda doesn't need to ask if I am feeling bad. She hugs me and I start to cry. We are headed deeper into Brooklyn. Past Park Slope to Minda's house. The cabbie is worried I will puke in his cab, so am I.

Minda and her husband, Andy, live in a brownstone with a backyard. She sets me up in her bed because it is nearest to the bathroom.

I am vomiting a lot. It is violent and accompanied by headaches. Finally it stops. Minda tucks me in. "Will you call and tell Dad I can't cook tomorrow?" I ask. Before I'm gone I ask Minda to tell Zack I'm sorry.

21.

A draft is coming through socks that are wedged between the air-conditioner and window sash. I pull the blanket over my head. Minda brings me oyster crackers and water. She tells me I've been asleep for seventeen hours, that she and Andy have slept on the futon. I thank her and fall back asleep.

I am awake and vomiting. Jason calls. I tell him I am very sick. He says he loves me and describes the patterned carpets that hide people's spills and vomit in Vegas casinos.

Minda asks if I need anything. I request bendy straws so I can drink easier, saltines, and ginger ale. She gives me a fresh T-shirt and boxer shorts.

22.

On the bedside table is a ginger ale with a bendy straw and some saltines. Minda wants to know how I am doing. I ask her to call Howard.

Howard is a friend of Minda's who lives in Maryland. He is soft-spoken and enjoys watching cartoons despite being an adult and a doctor. Howard doesn't really want to give advice without seeing me. But Minda is Minda. She gets Howard to give some: Don't let her get dehydrated. Lots of water. Pepto-Bismol tablets might help. If she starts vomiting blood, get her to the hospital.

It is night. All day I've been puking, sleeping, and drinking enough water to flush out a kidney stone. Minda brings me Pepto-Bismol tablets and a bowl of tiny star-shaped pasta.

23.

The sun is up and so am I. I sit in bed against a ramp of pillows and check e-mail. I have fifteen orders for novelties. Someone has blogged about my online store. I should be happy. I'm not. I'm overwhelmed. I only keep a small supply of my novelties in New York. I will have to go to my home base, in Scranton, PA, to fill the orders.

The craft magazine illo is a slam dunk. A friend has written to thank me for the pads with her name printed on them. She says the package looked phenomenal, as if it traveled on the back of a donkey.

Jason sent me an e-mail last night asking if I wanted to video chat. The city-themed hotel has the fastest Internet he has ever seen. I send an e-mail back saying I'm feeling better and tell him I need to go to Scranton.

Minda finds me flopped on the bed working on the donut illo. She stops me mid-doodle and makes me take a nap.

It's dark. I feel BETTER. Whatever was in me is gone.

Minda is typing away at her laptop, Andy is reading a book. There are overstuffed bookshelves lining the room. I scan the titles. How did Minda and I both end up with husbands who own *An Anecdoted Topography of Chance*?

Andy's

I thank Andy for sleeping on the futon. He mumbles. I think he said, "It wasn't anything. No problem." But he might have said, "I fucking hate people."

Andy is sending out bad-mood signals. I try to cheer him up by giving a detailed account of how the Canadian chain of Tim Horton's is trying to conquer the American donut market. It is the only thing I have learned in the fog of the last four days.

I explain that I want to use Timbits in the illo somehow. Timbits are Tim Horton's version of "Munchkins," i.e., donut holes. Andy knows Tim Horton's well; his mood lifts as he suggests to me that chocolate Timbits look like cat shit.

Minda goes to the kitchen and brings me a ginger ale with a bendy straw and another bowl of tiny pasta.

My sister offers to drive me home. I thank her but assure her I can take a taxi. She hugs me and tells me she loves me. She does not want me to leave. I feel very lucky and I am tempted to stay. This is because I know as soon as I leave, Minda and Andy will make fun of me for traveling to India.

I call Minda from the lobby as promised. Upstairs, I change the sheets and pillowcases. I set up at my desk and try to come up with an idea for the job. The idea happens. I will need Jason to finish it.

I do illos in different styles, depending on the idea. Often my idea is best as a drawing, but sometimes the idea needs to be built and photographed. I e-mail Una to apologize for the long pause and tell her an idea is on the way.

I hear the door unlock. It's Jason. I run at him like a puppy.

Jason's

24.

On the way out of the city we stop by a new Tim Horton's and buy forty chocolate Timbits.

There is an old Italian grocery shop near the Lincoln Tunnel. Jason circles the block. I enter the sandwich shop at the same time as a redheaded woman. An old lady behind the counter greets us. "What do you want?" she asks. "A sandwich to go," I say. The redhead says she is just looking. The old woman tells the redhead, "That's not what this place is for." The redhead continues to look around.

The old woman tells her to leave, to get out, to scram. The redhead protests. "Why can't I just look around?"
"It's a deli," I say, "not a museum."

That is my father's line. I'm surprised to hear it come from my mouth. This shop is a museum. It looks straight out of 1900 and reminds me of the store I grew up in.

The redhead is taken aback. The old woman behind the counter glows and thanks me sincerely. She makes my sandwich and asks if I'm from New York. I tell her I am. "I knew it," she says.

I hop in the car with the sandwich. An hour or so later, we are parked at the Delaware Water Gap, the halfway point to Scranton. The picnic tables by the river are covered in snow. We eat in the car. I lay napkins on our laps and hand Jason his half.

I'm happy to see our house standing. We have a mound of mail. Jason has sent me postcards from India and Las Vegas. We unload our bags and immediately go out to buy groceries. On the way, we stop at the library to take out some movies. It is in an old building modeled after a French monastery. The library is open till 9 p.m. most nights. Almost every film by Werner Herzog and Akira Kurosawa can be found on the shelves. They have books too.

Jason pushes the cart. He calls it a "buggy." This and calling any kind of soda "Coke" are all that's left of his Southern accent.

People study meditation for twenty years to clear their minds of worry and distraction. Jason and I go to Wegman's.

The first stop is always produce. Jason gets the standards. Green beans, Fuji apples, baby carrots, and so on. I find the curve-balls like fennel or beets. The fish department has misters in the cases. We hold hands and pick out a salmon fillet because it has omega-3. I remember we need peanut butter and am rewarded with a kiss. This ritual takes an hour, costs $125, and will feed us for the week.

Wegman's and the library were the first things that made me fall for Scranton. A love that slowly grows as Scranton continues to reveal its secrets. The giant lump of anthracite coal that wears a Santa hat at Christmas. A chain of ice cream parlors run by a family dairy. The post office branch located in the mall that is open later than all the others. The warning from our neighbor that he will blast a Civil War cannon at 11:59 on New Year's Eve. The unassuming farmer's market that has been going since 1939. Where a vendor started his recipe for squash by hitting it with a hammer. I'm not sure what the people of Scranton do for a living. I know there is a ring-pop factory. A place that makes scaffolding and a cardboard box company. There is also a landfill and a scrapyard.

Scranton

Tetris

I put away the groceries and make us coffee. Our home is a brick carriage house that was built in 1881. The place was an empty shell when we bought it. Jason is handy, so we did most of the renovation ourselves. We spent two months waking up at 6 a.m. and working till 10 p.m. The work was hard and dirty. My boogers were black the whole time. Every now and then we stopped to earn a living or get ice cream. We built a few secrets into the house like the Tetris drawers that accommodate the sink.

In the basement there's a darkroom, silkscreen setup, letterpress, sewing machine, wood tools, workbenches, shipping supplies, flat files, and a washing machine. I also keep my novelties down there. Most of them were made in our basement. I go down and pack up the new orders.

Jason has brought gifts back from Vegas. A pair of socks and three kinds of rocks that grow crystals. I make dinner while he reads the instructions for the rocks.

WARNING:
Eating rocks may lead to broken teeth!

The rocks are set up in bowls of water and vinegar. We add blue food coloring to one bowl, hoping to tint the "popcorn rock."

After dinner, I make bread dough that will rise overnight. Jason soaps the dishes and I rinse.

We watch *Paper Moon*. A black-and-white film shot in 1973. It's beautiful. I am so glad not to be puking.

25.

I put on my boots and walk down the hill to the post office. There is a line of people. The postman behind the desk recognizes me. "Those all set, honey?" he asks.

"Yup," I answer.

"You can just put them over there."

"Thanks," I say and pile the packages on the empty desk next to him.

I try to stack the round donut balls into a pyramid. It looks good, until it collapses. I wanted to make a novelty item for my store once, a matchbox set of miniature pickup sticks. It didn't work out, but the colored toothpicks are ideal reinforcement for my pyramid of Timbits.

I set up our photo lights and call Jason down. He says the pyramid doesn't get the idea across, that I need to add something, then goes back upstairs. An art director has requested images from him for a book cover. Jason is looking through his past contact sheets for photos of deserts that resonate.

The bread dough is ready to bake. I shape it into baguettes and place it in the oven. Part of my birthright is kitchen supplies. I set one of my father's gifts for fifteen minutes.

Una has e-mailed me the headline for the story: "The Donut Offensive." It matches my idea of Timbits as cannonballs perfectly.

Dr. Williams's office calls. My blood test was normal. He has mailed me the report and wants to make sure I show it to the neurologist.

Kitchen timer

A godawful buzzer goes off. The bread is done. I take it out of the oven and let it cool. I design and construct a prop cannon using the Timbits box.

Jason adjusts the lights and sets up the background paper. He gets out our digital camera and takes a photo. Deleting and reshooting follow with a lot of fussing. I e-mail the photo to Una and ask her to please write back sooner than later. I am afraid the Timbits will go soggy.

We eat sandwiches on fresh-baked bread.

Una loves it, but they need a Canadian flag put in the shot. Jason has gone back to the desert search. I build a flag and lure him downstairs with a coffee.

The Timbits with the flag is reshot and then sent. Jason wants to break my pyramid apart. I will not let him till I hear from Una.

Jason has found a lecture on the Internet for us to watch. It asks the question "What is the shape of the universe?" The answer is so bad it's good. There is a 98% chance the universe is flat.

26.

Last Halloween I needed a tan jumpsuit for my costume. I found a website with free shipping for orders over fifty dollars. All the jumpsuits in my size were on clearance. So I bought six in different colors and fabric weights. These have become my Scranton uniform. I pick out a warm heavy one with a tiny blue pattern.

Jason wakes up. I make a big breakfast with hash browns and eggs. Afterwards I'm tired. I lie down and read a book till it is time to make lunch.

My neurologist appointment is tomorrow at 1:45 p.m. I've missed the afternoon bus to New York. I did it on purpose. I want to stay here in my jumpsuit.

Una writes with good news. The donut job is done. Jason immediately eats a two-day-old Timbit. I'm tired and lie down.

Timbits

27.

It is 6 a.m. Jason rousts me out of bed and drives me to the bus
station. The morning bus is always packed and isn't direct. I like
the Friday-night bus. A different company operates it. The ride is
an hour shorter and ten dollars cheaper. It's rarely crowded. There
are a few drawbacks. Sometimes it smells like french fries and
once a driver took the bus to Newark instead of New York. He
was Jamaican and said "Sorry, mon" to the whole bus.

I fall asleep and wake up as we reach the city. I almost fall asleep
on the subway too. The mailbox at our Brooklyn studio is full.
Mixed in with the junk mail, I find my blood report and a postcard Jason sent us from India.

The Store is always busy on Fridays. Dad is happy to see me. Zack is even happier. My father's leg is swollen to the size and shape of Italy. They are buried in checks. My dad sits down and I take his place in front of the griddle. I throw down some pancakes. Zack tells me about the fight he and my father had this morning.

Zack was so mad he threw a slotted spoon. The dish washer made them both stop fighting and look: the spoon had ricocheted off the wall and it was balanced like a seesaw on the edge of the sink. Zack was in awe. My dad was so mad he said he wouldn't look, but Zack caught him peeking.

Zack and I kick ass in the kitchen. The food comes out perfect and fast. I stay till the lunch orders start. Zack gives me a high five as I leave.

The last time I was here I was having frequent migraine head-aches that destroyed me. I spent hours lying in the dark with a damp washcloth over my forehead, crying. The washcloth would drip down my cheeks. I'd distract myself by trying to figure out which were drips and which were tears. Dr. Schorr told me they were stress headaches and gave me a free sample of a headache medicine with a prescription.

My dad has always been indestructible. He never got sick or wore a coat in winter. Around when my headaches started, he didn't seem as invincible. He got a cold. His leg was giving him prob-lems. He and I have done the *New York Times* crossword semi-regularly since I was fourteen. When I would call him to do a puzzle he was too tired. I started having nightmares about him dying. A few times I collapsed in a sobbing puddle at the thought of it. Then my father started taking better care of himself, and my headaches got further apart. Soon, I only got a migraine once a month like I'd always had.

The nurse takes me in for an EEG. On the wall is a poster from a drug company. It lists famous people with epilepsy: Napoleon, Isaac Newton, Julius Caesar, and Socrates. The poster kind of makes me want epilepsy. The nurse puts a cap covered in electrodes on my head. She tries for half an hour to put gel into each electrode, most times the gel doesn't leave the tube. This office does not instill confidence. I think about leaving but remember I took a 6:30 a.m. bus to come here.

I am sitting in the doctor's office. There is a large bookshelf decorated with puppets and puzzles. A bright yellow copy of *Depression for Dummies* is wedged between some respectable-looking books.

Dr. Schorr comes in. He looks so much like Sigmund Freud it has to be on purpose. My file is in his hand. He glances at it. With a Yiddish accent he pretends to remember me. "I've seen ewe before. In April? Am I right?" He interviews me for five minutes at his desk.

We move to an exam room. I tell him about the food poisoning and show him the blood results from Dr. Williams. Dr. Schorr tells me, "Zese results are great. Ewe are in good shape. Your blood iz perfect." He looks at my EEG. "Ewe have a beautiful brain, my dear," he says, stroking his white beard.

The diagnosis is exertion headaches. "Don't worry, dear, these headaches are normal. Zhey are simply another kind of migraine. A little rare in woman. Zee headaches are more often found in men. Usually when zey ejaculate," Dr. Schorr says as he gives me a prescription and a free sample of a headache medicine.

Untitled page from the Berkeley Album, 1867–71

The Metropolitan Museum of Art is open late on Fridays. I enter the great hall with its supersized floral arrangements and receive my metal button.

The Met is a labyrinth. I've gotten lost too many times before. I ask the guards for directions to the exhibit "Playing with Pictures." The introductory paragraph silkscreened on the wall teaches me that photography became more accessible in 1854. This spawned a trend of people trading photos like baseball cards. Well-to-do women with time on their hands started cutting up these photos and making what were perhaps the first photo collages.

The exhibit is a manageable size. The show is made from pages of Victorian scrapbooks. Photo portraits have been cut out and pasted onto humorous watercolors. The collages are amusing and intricate. Heads are juggled or put on animal bodies.

I ask another guard where I can find Romare Bearden's *The Block*.

The Block is a giant photo collage of Lenox Avenue in Harlem. Bearden made it in 1971 after looking out the window of his friend's apartment. Brightly colored and chock-full of action. The thing is six feet long. I love it.

Our studio's windows are fogged up. Jason calls. It is snowing in Scranton. He has accepted a job from a health magazine that wants us to do a photo-illustration.

Work is easier when Jason is approached. Less pressure. The job is more about collaboration than brain fart. What and how to render is gently coaxed out together instead of the mental ping-pong that of late gives me headaches.

We do a monthly photo-illustration for the *New York Times Magazine's* food section. The column is called "Cooking with Dexter." It is about the writer's four-year-old chef. Jason and I have gotten so in tune on the job that every "Dexter" is like a date. From the brainstorming to the final art we hold hands.

One "Dexter" recipe was for cracklings. Our idea required a tunnel of lard. The fat kept flopping flat and leaving grease on the backdrop. Invisible thread was created to magically levitate dollar bills and sew multicolor quilts. I used it to sew invisible struts into the white flesh. My suturing did the trick, but Jason was totally grossed out and wouldn't hold my hand for a while.

The article is called "Suspicious Minds." I print out the story to read and scribble on. My eyelids are heavy. I brush my teeth and turn off the lights.

"Cooking with Dexter: Little House in the Hood"
The New York Times Magazine

Take five

28.

I wake up sluggish and dizzy. The subway is so fast, I hardly get halfway through the "Suspicious Minds" article. The story is about overreacting to your symptoms. Just because you have a twitching muscle doesn't mean you have Lou Gehrig's disease. That pain under your armpit, probably not lymphoma.

I get to The Store at 8 a.m. My father's in a good mood, though his leg is still messed up. I make myself breakfast while Zack sets up the kitchen. Regulars start filing in.

Out of the gate we are packed. It's hot and fast. I love it. I'm sad I missed last week. Zack looks out the kitchen door. There is a line of customers waiting to eat. "Holy shit," Zack says, "that is the best-looking senior female I have ever seen. I'm sorry, I would totally bang her." Zack doesn't shut up while we cook. Ever. At first I couldn't stand it, but now I find it comforting. I look at the line. She is an athletic, bronzed sixty-year-old wearing a cable-knit sweater. Zack calls to Luke, "This is the first woman over forty I'm hot for. Check her out." Luke is Zack's best friend and the waiter. He likes heavy metal and works out. "Not my type," Luke says. "She's all yours."

It's been going nonstop all morning. We get some giant checks with combo plates. My dad joins us despite his throbbing leg.

"What is with all the slotted spatulas? I'm gonna fucking throw them all out," my father says.
"Fucking Mara," Zack says, smiling.
"Dad, you're right. Throw them all out. That will show me. I deserve it. Teach me a fucking lesson."
Zack is laughing.
"Fuck you both," my dad mutters.

I am cooking four items at once and telling my father what types of pancakes to cook. Zack is manning the fryer and making an order of banana ebelskivers. I take my pans off the flames and pull out the broiler tray so I don't burn my toast. I lean on the cutting board and pause. My father asks what's wrong. I tell him I feel light-headed. He has Luke bring me water and tells me to sit down. He and Zack can finish my items.

I sit down in my father's orthopedic chair and close my eyes. "You alright, Mara?" my brother Zack asks.
"Yeah, just gonna sit down for a little."

I wake up from a catnap. "You give up?" I hear Luke ask the Canadian Olympic downhill skier with the lips my dad tells me about every time she's in.

"You give up?" is Luke for "Would you like the check?" My father is shouting through the pickup window. Zack is making another order of ebelskivers. I get up and join the line like nothing happened. I take over my father's items and he sits down.

"You okay?" my dad yells.
"I don't know. How's your leg?" I yell back.
"Not great," my father shouts.

We close early. It has nothing to do with my dizzy spell. That is just how The Store rolls. Zack and I bump fists. I make a sandwich and wrap it in foil. I wave good-bye to the whole store and head for Port Authority.

Port Authority bus terminal has banks of pay phones and a monument to Ralph Kramden. It reminds me of the city I knew as a kid. Dirty and funky. Not gold-plated and sanitized. Part of me loves it here. The other part of me is scared I've caught crabs from the bathroom.

Houseplants decorate the ticket office. Someone has a passion. Clip lights are pointed at ferns and ficuses. There is only one teller open.

I pass a food stall called Snacks and Wheels. They have 3-D signage shaped like tires. Someone has stolen the hubcaps from two of the wheels.

At my gate is a small line of people. Some sitting on the floor, others standing. I join the people of the floor. I'm not hungry but I eat my sandwich so I won't be stuck with the trash the whole ride.

My bus arrives and the people of the floor rise. It is not crowded. We all get a row. I curl up and set an alarm on my phone.

The alarm is the sound cartoon computers make when they fail. I call Jason and tell him I am near. The bus passes the library and civic pride washes over me.

Downtown

Jason picks me up at the bus stop. He kisses me and carries my bag to the car. Scranton is covered in snow. Some people's Christmas lights are still up even though it's February.

At home, Jason shows me the crystals that have started to form on the rocks. I'm introduced to a photographer named Greg. He is using our spiral binder to make a small-edition book. Greg is visiting from Rochester, New York, the birthplace of Wegman's. Our friend Gus is up for a short visit from the city too. He is tall and has to fold in half to hug me.

It is nice to have our house so full. I'm beat and stink from The Store. I take a bath and almost fall asleep in the tub.

29.

Jason's nephew Grant has a school assignment to give a report on the Gold Rush, dressed as John Sutter. Grant has requested we make his costume. Jason needs to mail it out to Atlanta tomorrow. We have not started.

Jason pulls *L'Or* by Blaise Cendrars off our bookshelf for inspiration. We brainstorm over coffee. It is the same sort of brainstorming I do for a living, but I'm slow to come up with ideas. Eventually we reach a consensus. The costume should be a simple T-shirt spatter-painted with gold, and there should be lots of fun accessories. We decide to spray-paint rocks to make gold nuggets. I will design and print business cards for Grant to give out that say

JOHN SUTTER • THE ORIGINAL GOLD-DIGGER

The next step is to forage at the crafts store.

We wander around the store looking for gold. Jason is inspired by everything. Gold pipe cleaners become souvenir bracelets Grant can give out. A pack of glitter can turn a saltshaker into a gold dust sprinkler. It is hard to keep up.

Jason is frustrated with my lack of enthusiasm and gives me the cold shoulder. I am perplexed at it myself and feel relieved when we check out.

At home Jason is excited to get started. He asks what task I want to do? I tell him I want to go to bed.

"What is going on with you, Beach Ball? Are you depressed?"
"I'm just tired."
"Lately, you are always tired."
"I don't feel like spray-painting things gold."
"That just doesn't sound like you. What is going on?"
"I feel nauseous."
"Is this physical or psychological?"
"Physical."
"Are you sure?"
Jason is waiting for an answer.

"It is physical. It really is," I say, and start bawling. Jason hates it when I cry. Not in a sweet "Don't wanna to see you cry, honey" way. More in a "That isn't going to help anything" Spock way.

He holds me though and kisses me on the top of my head. I tell him he is right: I normally do like spray-painting things gold.

I run to the bathroom and start barfing. Every time I throw up, a migraine headache swells.

Jason tucks me in bed and tells me he will take me to the walk-in clinic tomorrow morning. He sits on the edge of the bed asking me questions. He wants to write down all my symptoms, so we don't forget anything.

Jason uses a ruler to draw up a calendar of when I have been sick. He includes when I got food poisoning in India. The calendar, blood report, and symptom list is paper-clipped together, forming my sickness FAQ.

He gives me water, and I drink it all. I'm scared of getting dehydrated. I ask that two more glasses be put on the nightstand.

It is dark. Jason pours a small velvet drawstring bag into my hand. He has spray-painted the rocks. They look just like gold nuggets. I want to tell him we are going to be rich, but I am overcome by a bout of barfing. The headaches are the worst part.

30.

Jason gently wakes me. I have slept for sixteen hours. He wants to take me to the doctor. There is a local plumber who holds packages for us. His secretary's name is Jean. She has a little dog that barks and pees on the rug when we come to pick up our packages. Last time Jason was there he asked Jean who her doctor was. Jean said she wouldn't recommend her doctor, but that her friend loved this new walk-in clinic in Dunmore.

I'm ready. Jason calls me by my pet name and tells me I look homeless. He picks out clothes to replace my nightshirt and sweatpants. A crisp button-down and cream-colored corduroy pants. I haven't dressed this nice since a wedding we went to over the summer in Vermont. I can't really walk straight. Jason helps me down the stairs and into the car.

The clinic is barely ten minutes away. I have won the lottery. The waiting room looks brand new. In no time a nurse is taking my vitals.

The doctor is an old woman who resembles Mrs. Santa Claus. Jason tells her my symptoms and shows her the calendar. All she seems to hear is vomiting, fatigue, headaches.

She thinks I am pregnant. I tell her I just had my period. Dr. Claus says that doesn't matter. Odd. I thought it kind of did. She leaves and says she will return after the nurse has visited.

A nurse comes in and takes my blood. He leads me across the hall and gives me a cup to pee in. There is no sink in the bathroom. The nurse says this is because they do drug testing here and this prevents people from diluting their urine.

Not sure why, but I want a boy. Jason thinks a girl could be good because they are more low-key. He has a point. The brief fancy is gone. If I am pregnant the baby is in trouble. I've lost, not gained, weight. I can't be pregnant. Jason agrees.

Dr. Claus reenters. Jason tries to explain my symptoms again. She winks at him and tells us to come back tomorrow morning for the test results.

Jason puts some Pepto-Bismol tablets on my nightstand with a few saltines, and fills all my glasses of water. We remember the "Suspicious Minds" job and decide to try and work on it.

I read the rest of the article. One of the items is "Sudden, piercing headache probably not a big deal." This comforts me. Jason sets himself up near my sickbed and we brainstorm.

We go nowhere. I get a sudden, piercing headache and head for the toilet. What the hell am I puking out? I lie down completely depleted. Jason decides we need to bail on the job.

Nightshirt

31.

I can hear Jason working downstairs. I am sprawled out like melted cheese. My insides are empty. I try to rise, but a pain grows in my head that forces me back down. The pain snowballs as I begin to sob.

Fear propels me out of bed. I nearly fall over pulling on a pair of loose-fitting jeans. "Jase, we need to go to the doctor," I yell. "Help me down the stairs."

Jason is full of energy. I am a handful of dead batteries. He looks me up and down. "Beach Ball," he starts. "I'm not changing clothes. I can't." I fall onto him.

The wait time is just ten minutes at the walk-in clinic. A nurse takes my vitals and leads us to exam room 4.

A different doctor comes in than yesterday. She is younger with cropped hair and a solid build. Her name is Dr. Eget. "How did the test go? Is she pregnant?" Jason asks.

I am not pregnant. Dr. Eget apologizes, she needs us to start from scratch. We bring out my sickness FAQ.

Jason goes over the calendar. Dr. Eget makes him add more detail. The long version of events unfold. Dr. Eget nods her head and listens. She becomes privy to our travels and family obligations. I use all my might to make pleasant jokes.

Now Dr. Eget listens to my heart and hits my knee with a hammer. She has me stick out my tongue. It is black. "Is that a bad sign?" Jason asks, and grabs hold of my hand.

"I don't think so," Dr. Eget answers as she goes over my tests from yesterday.

It is official, I am starving. All the other results are normal. "We'll take a stomach X-ray now and move on from there. I'll be back soon," Dr. Eget says.

I tell Jason giraffes have black tongues too and ask why this room's lights are so bright. Jason starts fiddling with my iPhone.

I am escorted down the hall like a prisoner, only slower. The nurse asks me if I am pregnant. I tell her I am not. She hides behind a lead curtain and pushes a button.

Paper crinkles under me. Jason reads a message board off my phone. He quotes comments from "Lori," "Cynthia Blue," and "anonymous coward." We learn my black tongue likely comes from Pepto-Bismol and never to eat at the Burger King in the Cancún airport.

Dr. Eget returns. According to the X-ray my stomach is slightly folded, but shouldn't be causing this much trouble. Dr. Eget wants me to get a CAT scan of my brain and stomach. She has made me an appointment for 1:00 p.m.

"Can you tell us what is wrong?" Jason asks. "I'll know more after the CAT scan. In the meantime I'm going to give her some medicine that should help her keep food down," Dr. Eget says, handing us some slips of paper. Jason takes the prescriptions and in unison we thank her.

I optimistically shop for lunch on the two shelves that have food. Canned soup with pasta pearls and Fig Newtons. I am way more excited about lunch than Jason. The pharmacist rings our purchases up and warns us about the huge blizzard that is supposed to hit this afternoon.

Jason helps me into the car. I am pale and match the snow that has begun to fall. I put the little yellow pill on my tongue and let it dissolve. I should be able to eat in fifteen minutes.

"I love her. Can you believe how much time she spent with us? I've never talked to a doctor that long," I say to Jason in between small spoonfuls of soup.

"This is disgusting," Jason says.
"It's not so bad if you don't eat the chicken."
"How do you feel?"
"It is totally staying down."

We have driven past the medical imaging lab a hundred times and never noticed it. Inside is another professional, welcoming waiting room that is empty.

The receptionist tells me I can keep the pen and they will call me in a minute. The pen is quite nice. I thank her for fitting me in, and for the pen. She explains they had cancellations due to the snow, that senior citizens don't take chances. She offers me another free pen.

Jason is singularly focused. There is a TV on the wall showing a soap opera. A rich woman is confronting an evil doll. We don't have a TV. It isn't beneath us, we just wouldn't get any work done. I only get to watch five minutes. The receptionist calls my name.

A technician in pink scrubs ushers me into a dark room. The equipment has a new-car smell. For a second I think I have discovered a pint-sized *Stargate* that will transport me to distant galaxies. No, it is just the CT scanner.

The technician asks if I'm pregnant. Why don't these people talk to each other? She has me lie down and tells me to try not to breathe.

She hides in a little room and pushes some buttons. The cot and I pass through the circle in under thirty seconds. It takes longer to scan a drawing than my insides.

The technician helps me up and walks me to the waiting room. Despite energy from the pasta pearls I am unsteady on my feet. Jason's eyes are still fixed on the TV. The evil doll has just shot an old man. "Jase. Jason," I call. Jason looks up. "Wow, that was fast," he says as the technician hands me off.

The snow is sticking now. "Did you see her face?" Jason says as he helps me into the car. "Whose face?" I ask.

"The woman who brought you out."

"No."

"She looked terrified."

"Maybe it was that guy being shot on the soap. That place was amazing. Do you know how long I would have had to wait in the city? Oh my God, the CT scanner was just out of the box."

"I know. Scranton is showing off some of its secrets today."

I take a bath and put on clean clothes that can be worn in public.

We have two comfy chairs, I sit in one with a magazine and a plate of Fig Newtons. Jason sits in the other with his computer, typing. Snow is falling outside in pace with his keystrokes.

My phone rings. It is Dr. Eget. "Are you home?" she asks.
"Yes and I'm fed!" I reply. Jason comes stand beside me to eavesdrop.
"Are you sitting down?" she asks.
"Yes."
"Tamara, I just got the CAT scan results. There is a mass in your brain. It is very serious."
"What is it, Beach Ball? Is it okay?" Jason asks.
I nod my head no.
"I've been trying to call your doctor but he doesn't answer. Do you know another way to reach him?"
"I don't have any other number. I'm sorry. I need to give you to my husband." I hand the phone to Jason.

We stand close together in a tangle. Jason recounts what Dr. Eget has told him. The mass in my head is very large. It is the cause of my vomiting and headaches. A CAT scan is crude and can't distinguish between soft tissue. As a result they can't tell how much of the mass is tumor and how much of it is swelling. An MRI can tell the difference. Dr. Eget is going to call a local neurologist she trusts and try to get him to look at the CAT scan.

I am going to die. These things happen. My mom got this same sort of call. She went to the hospital and was gone in the same night. I'm okay with it. Jason is not. He is more upset than I have ever seen. I think he is going to puke. I am calm, but to be fair, I have been puking for three days straight. I wish my mom had met Jason.

I-love-yous are followed by vise grip hugs. I tell Jason I have no regrets, if I had to do it over I'd do it the same. He is horrified by this and begins to cry. I kiss him and ask him to call my sister and father.

Jason describes it to her as "scary news." As he continues to speak I can tell my sister is falling apart. Jason hands me the phone. I tell her I love her and she says the same.

Jason is surprised at how untroubled my dad is by the scary news. He hands me the phone and I tell my father I love him, that I have no regrets, no changes, it's okay, I'm ready, I want him to know I love cooking with him and Zack. My father tells me he loves me and loves cooking with me, in the same voice he does every Saturday. It's clear my dad hasn't registered what Jason said.

It is so quiet. The heater cycles on. Jason puts his chin in my eye. It is my favorite thing. He uses it much more sparingly than I use milking his arms. Sometimes when he hugs me I stand on tippy toes and steal some chin. As soon as he realizes what has happened, Jason will yank his chin out from below my brow and say, "Not cool!"

Our phones ring. I go into the bathroom so we don't interrupt each other.

"Mara, what is going on? Minda is freaked the fuck out," my father asks as I shut the door and sit on the toilet.
"Not sure. They found a mass in my head. It is large—they don't know how much of it is tumor yet."
"Is there anything I can do?"
"Do you know any neurologists or neurosurgeons?"
"No."
"Are you sure wasn't there one from California who surfed?"
"Wait, there was one. What was his name? Shit."
"Duncan."
"Yes, Duncan McBride."
"Can you ask him for a recommendation?"
"I'll try."
I tell him I love him and he says the same in a different voice than before.

Jason is still on the phone. He cups his hand over the mouthpiece and whispers to me, "It's Eugene. He is going to help us. Don't worry." I don't know what to make of this.

Eugene has known my family since I was little. He started as a regular in The Store. I'm not sure what Eugene did, but my dad decided he was too demanding and banned him from coming to The Store. He banned Eugene for life.

After a year, Eugene started to call every so often and politely ask, "Can I come back now?" My father would say, "No. Sorry, it is for life." Eugene would call next month and say "How about now?" One day Eugene did this and my father responded with "Please come back. I miss you." This is the moment Eugene became embedded in our lives.

Minda works for his film company. I assume she is the reason he knows. I can picture his concerned eyes watching her dissemble. He's a noble man, the definition of altruistic. Minda has worked tirelessly for him for just shy of a decade. She loves him and believes in the civic-minded films they make together. But she wouldn't argue if I said my father was right to ban him. Eugene is impressively demanding. I am afraid he will get me banned from some amazing neurosurgeon.

Per Eugene's instructions, Jason calls the digital imaging lab and gets my CT report sent to us.

It turns out Eugene's sister-in-law had brain surgery last year. Eugene points out to Jason, his pain is our gain.

The Scranton imaging lab is top-notch. Jason receives the CT report within five minutes of asking. He sends it on to Eugene, who plans to send it on to doctors in Pittsburgh, New York, and—the curveball—Germany.

The panel of doctors say I need to go to the emergency room. The mass is located on my brain stem. It is huge. They are afraid it will block the blood supply to my brain. Eugene is trying to figure out if I should go to Pittsburgh or New York. He is waiting to hear if the surgeon who saved his sister-in-law's life will accept me as a patient.

We are on hold. Jason starts to cry. I give him a hundred little kisses. This makes him cry more. Executive decision. I want to go to New York. I want to go now. Jason yields and begins to pack our things.

I get up slowly so I don't give myself a stroke. Jason shuts the water off and drains the pipes so they won't freeze. I look at the sink and envision Jason here alone opening our Tetris drawers. I'm not scared, but this makes me so sad.

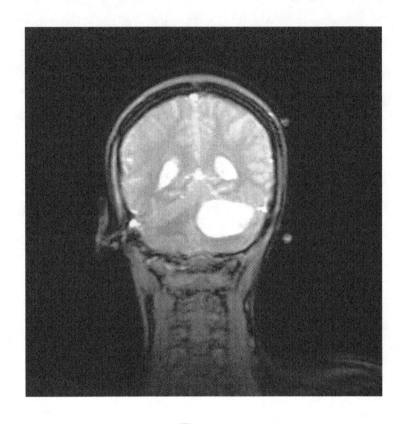

The mass

"We are on our way. That is great. Let me give you to Tamara. I need to merge," Jason says and hands me the phone.

"Hey, Eugene."
"How you doing?"
"I'm okay."
"Dr. Stieg is amazing. The best."
"Thank you. That helps. Jason wants to know where we are going?"
"New York Presbyterian Hospital. The entrance is at Sixty-eighth and York. There is valet parking. I'm still working on getting you an emergency MRI. I'll call back soon."
"We'll stand by." I hang up.

"Jason, Eugene is really kicking ass. The hospital has valet parking. That's a good sign, right? Do you think you tip the valet?"
"I think valet at a hospital is common. Yeah, we definitely should tip the attendant. Do you have some singles? Where am I going?"
"Sixty-eighth and York. I've got a fiver."

Jason says that the five will do and warns me he will need directions to the George Washington Bridge from my iPhone.

I'm fading. The roads haven't been plowed yet. The bulk of the traffic has collectively decided to drive only in the center lane. Jason starts to cry a little. I tell him everything is going to be okay. I say this but really don't think I am going to be here next week.

We slide down the exit ramp into the canopy of the Shell station. Jason goes to the bathroom. I open the car door and vomit. My head. I cry. Not because I am scared, but because it is so fucking painful.

Jason wakes me up. I've fallen asleep while he is pumping gas. "Can I just sleep till the Delaware Water Gap?" I ask.
"No. I don't want to worry that you've passed out. Dissolve another pill on your tongue and eat some more Fig Newtons."
"Hold on, don't pull out yet," I say as I open the car door and start throwing up.

Jason answers the phone. "That makes sense, I mean, she does have a childlike mind," I hear him say.

I used to babysit for a little girl who never wanted to eat. I'd cut her sandwiches into five strips. As she would eat each fifth of the sandwich I would hide a finger. By the end I was left with a fist. Her mother couldn't understand why she kept asking for ham sandwiches till I explained she was asking for hand sandwiches.

Jason relays the call to me. It was Dr. Eget checking in after talking to the local neurologist. He thinks I have a type of tumor typically only found in children. Dr. Eget says this is just a guess. I need to have an MRI ASAP. Jason thanks her and explains that we are driving to a New York hospital. I am worried that this has hurt her feelings. Jason says there is no way in hell he is letting me get brain surgery in Scranton.

I give my sister an update. She and I decide not to invite my father to the hospital. In a worst-case scenario, Eugene could get me banned from one rock star neurosurgeon. My dad, on the other hand, has the potential to get me blacklisted from every neurosurgeon in the tristate area. I ask Minda if I can call my brothers, Danny, Charlie, and Zack. I want to tell them I love them. She tells me I can't because it will scare them.

The roads are icy. Jason is driving as fast and slow as he can. My cell phone rings. Jason picks up and puts it on speakerphone. It is a conference call with Eugene and Dr. Stieg's assistant Amanda. "Hello, Jason. Can you hear me?" Amanda says. "Yes, Amanda. Hello," Jason replies.

"I couldn't get the emergency MRI for tonight, but I was able to schedule one at 8 a.m. It is really rare they do an emergency MRI and she isn't displaying emergency symptoms."

"I understand. Can you tell me what signs should I look for that this is an emergency?"

Amanda pauses. "Well . . . if she doesn't know where she is. If she starts to call things by the wrong word or doesn't know her name. If she falls unconscious."

Eugene interrupts. "Amanda. A neurosurgeon I know in Germany said that due to the size of the mass and its location, chances should not be taken. That an MRI should be given as soon as possible."

"Um . . . I understand your concerns. Let me call and voice them to radiology. I'll try to sway them." After a few thank-yous from us Amanda hangs up.

Eugene is still on the line. "I didn't like the way she answered your question. She hesitated. Do you have something to write with? I want to give you Dr. Stieg's cell phone number." I fumble in my bag and find a pen.

"So call him when you are half an hour away from the hospital. This way he can alert his team you are coming."

"Will do, Eugene. Thanks," Jason replies. Eugene hangs up.

"What are your brothers' names?" Jason asks.
"Danny, Charlie, Zack," I answer. "Nailed it, didn't I?"
"Yes, I love you." Jason says, and starts to tear up.
"I love you. It will be okay," I say.

"Can you call Dr. Stieg and check in?" Jason asks.

"I don't want to bug him. It seems rude."

Jason pleads, "Beach Ball, it's a brain tumor. This is his job." I dial Dr. Stieg.

"Hello, is this Dr. Stieg?"

"Yes, I'm Dr. Stieg." I hear a dog bark in the background.

"This is Tamara Shopsin. Um, we are half an hour away from the hospital."

"Okay, I'll let them know you are coming. Anything else?" Dr. Stieg says. I ask Jason.

"Directions," Jason answers.

"Really?" I whisper to Jason.

"Yes, do it," Jason orders.

"Um, sorry. Can you tell us the best way to get to the hospital from the GW Bridge?" Dr. Stieg gives easy and precise directions. I thank him and hang up.

We pass a sign that says "Triborough Bridge Renamed RFK Bridge." I freak out. Why would the city rename a bridge everyone knows? The name isn't even debatably offensive, like the Tomahawk Chop. Unless the city now finds logic offensive.

"It goes over three boroughs!" I shout.

"Calm down, Beach Ball. Focus. Tell me the rest of the directions. I need your help," Jason begs.

"Stieg's directions are different than my iPhone. Do we go with the brain surgeon or Google?"

"The brain surgeon."

New York peeks through suspension cables and snowflakes. Another pop quiz. I answer, "Miss Piggy, Gonzo, Fonzy, Kermit, Big Bird, Bert & Ernie, Statler & Waldorf."

Dr. Stieg's directions are perfect. We pull into the hospital's cul-de-sac and are met by a parking attendant with white gloves. I climb out of the car too fast and fall down. Jason takes my arm. A red carpet leads to a revolving door. It looks like the entrance to a hotel.

Minda pops out from nowhere and hugs me. "I didn't know you would be here," I say.
"I told you we were on our way."
"I'm tired. Oh hi, Andy. You came, too?" My perception of Andy is anchored by his hatred of celery and hospitals. He gives me a thumbs-up and smiles.

Minda holds me up as we sign in at the reception window. It's the same type of window they sell movie tickets through. We are told to take a seat.

"Are those lithographs by Sol LeWitt? No, they are rip-offs? I can't tell," I ask, pointing to squiggles on the wall. Andy confirms that they are signed by Sol LeWitt. The conversation flows easily. I drift in and out.

They call my name. I enter the ticket booth and fill out paperwork. I am put in a wheelchair. My cadre follows as a nurse pushes me to a room with walls made of curtains.

Minda helps me put on a gown decorated with snowflakes and footballs. A nurse lifts me gently by the armpit into a hospital bed.

Dr. Smith is from team Stieg. She wears a crisp white lab coat over a blouse and pleated pants. Her stethoscope is folded neatly into her pocket. She asks me a lot of questions. What's my name? Where are we? Have I been sensitive to smell, taste, sound, and light? I thought that was just India being India. Have I had trouble with balance? I slowly answer yes to almost all her questions.

I am asked to touch my nose and then the tip of her finger. I am on an episode of *Cops*. I can hear the theme song. We start with my right hand. She moves the finger after each time I touch my nose. Now I try with my left hand. I am much slower and miss her finger a bunch. I beg to try again. "You did really well. You can try again later," Dr. Smith says.

Dr. Smith warns if swelling continues, I will need a spinal tap to relieve the pressure in my brain. Jason and Minda learn more. I close my eyes.

Dr. Yi is my age and looks cool. Things are clipped to her green scrubs. She wears her stethoscope like an ascot. She is the emergency room's on-call doctor. Dr. Yi asks me the same questions as Dr. Smith. She plays the drunk test with me and I do worse, not better. I ask for water. Dr. Yi gives me some and says, "From here out you are NPO."

I am taken for a chest X-ray. This is hospital policy. No one thinks anything is wrong with my chest.

I have been fully admitted to the emergency room. They take away my private room and put me on a gurney. I am parked next to the nurses' station in the urgent care unit. A woman with a limp in a hospital gown is begging for change. She just needs a nickel. I tell her I have no pockets.

I am in good spirits. Jason stands next to me holding my hand. Andy has brought a book called *Hellraisers: The Inebriated Life and Times of Richard Burton, Richard Harris, Peter O'Toole, and Oliver Reed.*

I learn about the friendship of Keith Moon and Oliver Reed. The first time they met, Reed was taking a bath inside his mansion. He heard "an almighty roar" that scared him. So he went outside in a bathrobe, wielding his emergency antique sword. It turned out the sound was Keith Moon's helicopter.

Andy is interrupted. The woman with a limp has found her nickel. She passes by eating a bag of potato chips. I am starving. I ask Minda to get me something from the vending machine, ideally animal crackers.

"You are NPO," Andy says.

"What is NPO?" I ask.

"Nil Per Os, or nothing by mouth. You can't eat or drink," Andy answers.

Hellraisers

Andy wants to go home. He needs to prepare for a panel discussion on the use of avant-garde films in musical performance. He is moderating the panel tomorrow at the Goethe-Institut. Minda points out it will likely be canceled due to the huge snowstorm. She takes him to the other side of the hall.

They come back. Andy has decided to stay a bit longer. My sister looks as though she was crying. Oh my God, I am starving. My father calls. He has gotten in touch with Duncan, the neurosurgeon from California.

Duncan says Stieg is the best neurosurgeon in New York. Duncan also mentions he would have sent me to NYU hospital. TMI.

TAMARA SHOPSIN

I am wheeled to the basement at a clip by an orderly. Minda, Andy, and Jason try to keep up. The orderly leaves. There is no one down here. This floor is supposed to be closed. It is 10 p.m. Amanda and Eugene have won my emergency MRI. The schedule must have been full till closing. The technicians are staying late for me.

It is nice to be away from the beeping and moaning of the ER hallway. Andy resumes his story. Keith Moon steps out from the helicopter and introduces himself. Reed and Moon get along like a house on fire. They party for days. One night, halfway through dinner, Moon suggests that they play a game. The game turns out to be See if Oliver Reed Can Run Keith Moon Over. The game requires a car and a field.

A technician joins us. His name is Dennis. "There is no metal allowed in the MRI machine. Are you wearing any jewelry?" he asks.
"No, I'm not," I say.
"No wedding ring? No watch? Do you have a bullet stuck in you or an artificial joint? Have you ever worked for the Transit Department or in any kinda metalwork?"
"No," I answer.
"Transit Department. Why does that matter?" Jason asks.
The technician explains, "The MRI machine uses magnetic fields that will twist and attract metal. We have had a few people who worked grinding subway tracks. Dey didn't know it but tiny bits of metal had got in their eyes."
"Oh shit," Minda says.

Dennis wheels me into the MRI room. It looks like a '90s web-cam, except it hardly fits in the room and has a long table jutting out of where the lens should be. Dennis picks me up using my bedsheet as a taco shell and sets me down gently on the MRI table. My head is surrounded by curved pillows. He puts a head-band on me and a game show buzzer in my hand.

"Are you claustrophobic?" Dennis asks.

"No. I like small spaces," I say.

"That's good. It is going to take a half an hour and then you are going to do it again with contrast. I'm going to be right here. If you have any problems push this button. You can see out by look-ing up at this window on the headband. Try not to move your head. Be as still as you can. If you move, we gotta do it again. ¿*Comprende?* You ready?"

"Yeah, I'm ready."

I am loaded into the machine. I look up and can see my feet. There is a tilted mirror on the end of a stick that juts out of my headband. It is a simple periscope. I love it.

The machine makes loud noises. They sound like an airplane far-ting. I don't move. The sounds change. The technician radios to me in my tube. "All done. Good job," he says.

My cot slides out. "I'm going to put contrast in you now. This dyes your bloodstream so we can see the vessels in your brain," the technician says. I notice there is an IV connector sticking out of the crux of my arm. I don't remember it being put in. He pumps the contrast into my arm. "Man, that machine makes strange noises. At the end there it seemed to be saying, 'Get out. Get out. Get out.'"

Scale-model MRI

"Yeah, people always complain about the crazy noises. Ready to go in again?"

I'm sucked back in. I notice the machine is put together with plastic screws. I'm completely still. It is the same thing only the noises are different. He lowers me out. The machine is so loud. I tell him the noises this time reminded me of my apartment in Brooklyn. That I heard buses idling and truck brakes squeaking.

"I live in Brooklyn. Red Hook. I was raised there," Dennis says proudly.
"Never met anyone really from Red Hook. Are you still able to live there? I heard the rents went crazy."
"Oh yeah, it's nuts. My moms bought our building in like 'seventy-two. So we don't got any worries."
"That's awesome."

The orderly collects me. The hospital is huge. It is made up of different buildings connected by tunnels and ramps. We convoy back to the nurses' station. The orderly says, "This is the best spot in the hall. All the nurses keep an eye on you. Make sure you're all right." I'm not buying it.

Andy wants to leave. I don't blame him. Minda changes his mind. No one is checking on us anymore. Things seem to be slowing down. It is midnight. Word is the storm has arrived in full force outside. Jason is standing close to me. We hold hands and look at each other. Andy says the shift is changing. We will probably get another doctor soon.

I ask when I can eat. Dr. Sussman says not till after my surgery. I tell him I am starving. He says that feeling is something else. I am apparently heavily medicated right now. Dr. Sussman explains I shouldn't be hungry. I am being fed through an IV drip. I look up and there is a plastic bag on a stick connected to me. Like in *The Wizard of Oz*, my heart's desire has been there the whole time.

It is 2 a.m. Minda's well-verbalized concerns and Jason's quiet patience have gotten me a room. The nurse puts monitors on my chest and a new bag in my IV stand. I don't know what is in the bag, maybe water and sugar. I wonder if Capri Sun drink pouches were invented by someone who was sick. Minda and Jason are glad there is a monitor attached to me. This way when I fall asleep they will know I am not dying.

It is fun again. Andy tells us about the swordfight Keith and Oliver had. And the night Oliver showed Keith the porn film he shot with his girlfriend.

Minda and I lock pinkies. My twin sister is having a hard time. She is scared. I look at Jason and see he is scared too.

My roommate in the next bed over has a voice box. He has an attack. I hear fast beeping followed by a swarm of nurses and doctors. On a scale of 1 to 10, he is at 10. I said 9 when the doctors asked me. But now that I hear my roommate I realize I'm more like 8.

3 a.m., the results of my MRI. I have a hemangioblastoma. They give me steroids and say they will tell me more when my doctor arrives.

My roommate is taken away. There is a new nurse. Her name is Danielle. She has long black hair. I thought the other nurses were nice. I was wrong. Danielle brings us comfy chairs and pillows. We all fall asleep.

32.

Andy makes a breakfast run. It is snowing so hard, New York City schools are closed. I can remember the one time P.S. 3 had a snow day growing up. Us five kids went fucking nuts on Morton Street, pelting the crap out of each other. Thank God, we hadn't learned about hiding ice in snowballs yet. In between the free-for-alls we warmed up at The Store. I'd stand with my butt pressed against the steam table until my brother or sister stole my spot. Our mittens hung above the griddle with the bacon weights to dry. Except for Charlie's, because he had Freezy Freakies and was afraid they would melt.

Minda bites into a giant everything bagel and drinks orange juice. I ask her if I can have some—I give a beat and smile. Everybody laughs at this.

Dr. Zirk sports a white lab coat with a button-down shirt that looks like graph paper. He gives me a short interview and the drunk test. My reflexes are catlike on the right side and doglike on the left. Dr. Zirk speaks plainly so we can understand the findings of the MRI. Jason asks lots of questions. I try to stay awake.

The hemangioblastoma is located near my cerebellum on the left side of my brain. The tumor is small. Most of the mass is from a cyst that is the size of a chicken egg. This is why my left reflexes suck ass. The cerebellum controls balance and coordination. My bike is not broken. I am.

The steroids have so far kept the chicken egg from swelling further. This is why I haven't had a stroke yet or needed a spinal tap. My weekly bouts of vomiting were from the cyst swelling up and deflating. It wasn't India that tasted bad and smelled like shit. It was me. The headaches I have been getting are because there is not enough room in my skull to think.

They want to operate today. Dr. Stieg is going to stop by in an hour or so.

Dr. Zirk explains there are two surgeries to perform before the brain surgery. The first procedure is a cerebral angiogram. This will allow the doctors to make a map of the tiny vessels that supply blood to my tumor. The second surgery is called embolization. It blocks blood flow to the tumor. This makes removing the tumor less risky.

The final procedure will be the brain surgery. My skull will be broken. The tumor will be removed and the fluid will be drained from the cyst.

I thank Andy and tell him he should go get ready for his talk. I take it as a good sign that Minda lets him leave. I want her to call my brothers and tell them I love them. Tell them that I have no regrets. Minda has told them. She tears up. I make a note to myself to stop saying "I have no regrets." Jason is in the hallway calling his mom. There are kind people in Atlanta praying for me.

Dr. Stieg wears a white lab coat with his name embroidered in red. The same type of embroidery plumbers use on their uniforms. His eyes twinkle as he tells me, "Before you know it you will be walking, dancing, and skiing. You don't have anything to worry about. Do you have any questions or concerns?"

I don't have the heart to tell him I've never skied. "Sounds good to me," I say.
Jason and Minda ask questions. "Is her tumor benign?" "What are the risks?" "Will there be long-term effects?" "Are the other two surgeries dangerous?"

Dr. Stieg says, "Not sure if we are going to do the angiogram and embolization." He doesn't give a reason why.

I think it is because my tumor is so small, we don't need the two surgeries. But maybe it is because my cyst is so large, we don't have time for them? Maybe due to the snowstorm, there isn't enough staff? My wheels spin.

"One surgery is better than three," I say.
"Not necessarily," Dr. Stieg replies.

I am taken to the basement. A technician holding scissors and a razor approaches. She explains that she is going to shave spots all over my head. She pulls some green mounds out of her pocket that look like giant candy buttons and says, "I'm going to glue these to your head."

"Go for it," I say.

She pulls up a chair and starts carefully cutting and shaving. I ask what the dots are for.

The technician explains they are called fiducial markers and are being glued into a grid shape on my skull. The dots will show up as points in the MRI. The markers will stay glued on during surgery. They will be used to triangulate where my tumor is.

"You got any metal on you?" Dennis asks.

"No metal. I got dots," I say.

"Try not to itch 'em. You don't want them to move," Dennis warns as he helps me onto the MRI table.

"All done. Good job," Dennis radios to the tube. I am lowered out. He wheels me to the hall and asks what the machine said to me this time.

"LET'S GO METS, LET'S GO METS, LET'S GO METS!" I chant, raising my frail arms that are connected to tubes.

"Well, have a nice life," Dennis says.

Major fuckup, he is a Yankees fan.

We are back to the moans and beeps of the ER. Minda thinks the green knobs that cover my head are cyberpunk. Jason thinks they are more ankylosaurus. I think they are genius.

There was a misunderstanding. Dr. Zirk apologizes for the confusion. I am still slated to have the angiogram and the embolization. No reason is given. I wonder if the MRI with the dots showed that my cyst has started growing again.

"I'd like to explain the dangers associated with the procedures. Then I will need your signature that you understand the risks of the surgeries," Dr. Zirk says, and hands Jason a clipboard. I don't pay attention when he talks about the risks of the brain surgery. I'm more open to debate the need for the other two surgeries.

Fuck, shit, cock. To do the angiogram, a miniature tube is inserted into my thigh. Somehow it is run through a blood vessel all the way up to my brain. When it gets to my brain, a dye is released and an X-ray is taken. Then for the embolization, crazy glue is injected strategically into the vessel that feeds my tumor via my thigh.

The angiogram comes with rare cases of internal bleeding, severe allergic reactions, and stroke. The embolization has the same risks, but the chance of stroke is higher. Minda and Jason are scared by this. I want to do whatever the doctors recommend.

Jason reads the documents all the way through. He puts the pen in my hand and I sign them.

"Are you jealous?" I ask weakly, looking up at Minda.
She pauses. "Of you getting to ride in an elevator laying down?"
My sister understands me well.

The doors open. There is a flock of doctors in white coats. I hear
the anthem from *Top Gun*. Soon I realize they are all waiting for
me.

I sign something that allows them to share my operation with
students and medical equipment companies. Everyone shakes
Jason's hand and tells us their name. I am given a special introduction to the anesthesiologist named Peri, who slips something
into my IV.

"You ready? You okay?" Minda asks. My mouth tastes funny. I ask
to brush my teeth. Minda looks to Peri. "Of course. Just after the
operation," Peri says, pushing me away from my sister. I tell Peri
the brand name of toothpaste I use and that I prefer fresh mint
to cool mint.

Jason kisses me and says good-bye. I'm rolled away through the
type of doors that normally lead to a restaurant kitchen.

I'm on a metal table in the middle of the room. "Are you warm enough? Is the table too cold?" Peri asks.

"I'm okay."

"Good. I'm just going to shave your pubic hair."

"What? No you're not. Are you?"

"Yes. I'll leave a little in the middle. I need to do both sides in case they can't get in from the first side they try."

"I've never done that."

"I'll be careful. I do it all the time. How about I just shave a little first so you can see it doesn't hurt?"

She has left me a little Mohawk. It looks like a TV "censored" bar, but vertical.

Tools are passed around. I hear beeping. No clue what is going on, but shit is definitely going on.

"Good job. The angiogram is done. We are going to perform the embolization in another room," Peri says, and I'm hoisted back onto the gurney.

This room is even more high tech than the last. It seems like a natural setting to build a Mars Rover or assemble ink-jet cartridges. I am glad it doesn't feel like 1943.

Minda is trying not to cry. Jason kisses my forehead. I tell him the rooms were amazing and full of space-age equipment. He asks if they used all the equipment on me. I tell him I have no idea and realize I am speaking quite slowly. I close my eyes. It feels so good to close them. "They are going to do the last surgery now," Jason says. "Is there anything you need?" Minda asks. I hear myself ask for orange juice, a book on modular origami, and some solid-color squares of paper. I emphasize that the paper should have NO patterns.

The room is ready. There are so many people. They are gathered beside Dr. Stieg. I am introduced to a new anesthesiologist named Harry. He tells me I will be unconscious for the operation. I'm scared, more scared than I was to have my pubes shaved. Harry holds my hand and I count backwards.

Suck on this

I don't know where I am. My throat is closing in. Someone rubs a wet green sponge on a stick across my lips. The small amount of water is heaven. I'm not sure if I am able to speak anymore. "This is not the desert. Why am I so thirsty?" I rasp. No one answers me.

Now that I realize I can talk, I can't stop. There is an ugly painting of wildflowers on the wall. "Where am I? Is this de desert? But there are flowers. This can't be de desert. This can not."

A woman rubs the sponge on my lips some more. I make a slurping noise as I try to suck the water into my mouth. "Stop that. Just on the outside of your mouth," she scolds.

"What is all dat beeping? What am I wearing? Why won't nobody tell me? Sorry. I jus want to figure out where I am. Really sorry." I have apologized because I am afraid they will get annoyed and shoot me.

And then it hits. I know my name. I remember driving through the snow, Jason crying, valet parking, and Sol LeWitts. I know my throat hurts because I've had a tube shoved down it for hours. "I'm sorry. Yew are trying to help. I'll be quiet," I say. "Don't worry, honey. You did good," a nurse says, and rubs the sponge stick across my lips.

I can feel Minda's wet cheek and sharp pains. "I love you. Don't hug me cuz it hurts," I say meekly.

"What?" Minda says through snot and tears.

"Pleaze don't hug me cuz my neck. I'm okay, Minda. Don't cry."

They are surprised I can talk. Jason drags the green sponge stick across my lips. "I love you, and I love you," I say to Jason and Minda. "And I love you too, Andy. Thanks for being here. I'm . . . I'm sorry you always get the third 'I love you.'"

They burst out laughing. "What? He does," I say. I ask them to tell Dad I'm okay. They have. My brothers know too.

Now they are surprised I can't stop talking. I tell them what I remember from the surgery. How they put all these cords in me and I didn't know what any of them wuz for. That I was trying to learn all the first names and luckily the guy who gave me anesthesia had a really hairy beard and his name was Harry. And then how I don't remember anything. I can't shut up. They are laughing at me again.

Minda has oddly brought fresh squeezed orange juice and origami paper, though I'm not allowed to drink water yet.

They take turns dipping the sponge stick into a cup and dragging it across my mouth.

Dr. Smith appears. She was the very first doctor I saw here. I scream "Hey" like we were in a sorority together.

"How are you?" Dr. Smith asks.
"I'm fantastic. Look, I can wiggle 'em all!" I screech as I play an imaginary piano.
"That's excellent. Great."
"I'm dreaming of drinking a Big Gulp glass of water."
"You can."
"Everyone must be really annoyed with me 'cause I won't shut up."
Minda interrupts, "She said you can."

It tastes so good. Oh my God. Oh my God. My sister tells me, "No chugging," and pulls the straw away. I tell her I'm not chugging, I'm savoring, and open my mouth for her to put the straw back.

Dr. Smith asks, "Let me see how you're doing. Can you hold your arms up in the air?" I try to lift my arms but can't. "Um, derz all these wires," I say.

She unhooks some of the monitor cords and my IV. "That's fine. That's good, squeeze strong. Pull toward you. Touch my finger. Touch your nose. Excellent. Pick up this leg here. And the other," Dr. Smith says, almost breaking into applause.

We are celebrating that I can touch my nose and move my legs.

The patient in the next bed is being asked "Are you farting?" by a nurse. I look at Jason and smile. He chomps his teeth at me, which is code for I love you, I love you.

I drink some more water too fast and almost choke. "It's okay. Chill out and I'll give you more," Minda says, wiping my mouth.

"I was gonna be happy if you were just asleep, and I could feel you breathing. Do you know my name?" Minda asks. I say her first and last name. Then I say it again and include her middle name. She starts sobbing and hugs me.

My nurse's name is Taylor. She tells Minda, Jason, and Andy visiting hours are over. Minda wants to stay. Badly. I tell her she should get some rest. They all leave for Gloria's apartment. Eugene's mother, Gloria, is away. She is celebrating President's Week with her grandchildren. Her apartment is empty and three blocks away from the hospital. No shit.

Every five minutes is an emergency. Gagging, screaming, and breathing.

My machine is beeping fast. I'm in stupid pain. I call out for my nurse but no one answers. I start crying. A woman comes over and makes the beeping slow. She says Taylor is on break.

I am crying. It hurts to cry. I call for a long time. A nurse comes over. "I want to call my husband and sister. I want them to be here." Tears are streaming down my face.
"It's 3 a.m. Can you wait till 6 a.m.?" the nurse says.
"No. I want to call them now," I say. The nurse offers to get Dr. Smith.

Dr. Smith asks gently what is wrong. I tell her my neck and my throat and the sounds and nobody is watching me and nobody checks on me and my machine keeps going off.

The IV is in wrong. My arm is bleeding. Dr. Smith fixes it and the machine stops beeping. She gives me some medicine for the pain and asks the nurse why I don't have boots on. The nurse says I'm not hers.

Plastic boots that inflate in waves are put on my legs. Dr. Smith asks if I'm okay now. I tell her I think I am better, but start to cry and can't stop. Dr. Smith holds my hand and sits by my bed till I settle down.

I can't sleep. I try to count backwards because it worked in the surgeries. It is too loud. The sounds are disturbing. It is the sound of people dying. I can see them through the paper thin curtains. I am trying so hard not to cry. The plastic leg wraps are inflating and deflating around my calves. I think Jason would like the way it feels.

I have to go to the bathroom. I call out for a long time.

Taylor finally comes over. I tell her I'd like to use the restroom. "You have a catheter. You can just go, silly," Taylor says with a Southern accent.

Taylor changes the bag and shows it to me. "See, you peed a lot, honey."
"The other nurse said I could call my family at six a.m."
"You don't want to let them sleep? It's only five a.m.," Taylor says.
"I want to call them now."
"Sweetie, it's not visiting hours."

Minda answers on the first ring and is on her way.

Taylor fixes my gown that has been hanging open and cleans some blood off my arms.

33.

I look like shit. Minda apologizes nonstop for leaving. It is hard to speak but I tell her I was the stupid one who told her to go.

They should bottle the water here. Minda warns me to drink slower and pulls the straw away from my lips. A bouquet of fresh tulips is pulled out and placed beside me. I ask her what else is in the bag.

Toothpaste! Fresh mint, the kind I always use. A toothbrush is handed to me. It is messy. I miss the cup. I'm in paradise.

She has also brought an eye mask. I spoil her with compliments as she places it on me.

"Did you find this in the street?" I ask. No, she has bought it. Positive? Yes, definitely she bought it. Very difficult to find an eye mask at 5 a.m. in a snowstorm. Why does it smell so bad? A circle lit from behind floats in front of me. I push the mask off and it stops.

Minda puts the eye mask back on me. The circle appears again; it is filled with a chain-link fence of cells. It's onion skin. It is as if I am looking through a microscope. Now the slide changes and I'm looking at cells I scraped off the inside of my cheek with a toothpick when I was fourteen. The slides are changing too fast. I don't know what this is. Maybe pollen grains. I take the eye mask off and tell Minda it's magic.

At 7 a.m. there is a shift change. My new nurse is named Katrina. "Walking on Sunshine" by Katrina and the Waves gets stuck in my head. It's not annoying. It moves me that I am able to get a song stuck in my head. There are no windows. I know it is day because they have turned on the lights.

I put on the eye mask. Every kind of brush mop and broom I've ever seen flashes before me. I take the mask off and close my eyes. The brushes stop but there are M&M-colored scorpions dancing.

I ask Minda if she thinks the M&M scorpions I see are a new issue or a side effect of the magic stink mask. Minda says she is sorry that the eye mask smells so bad.

"Can I call Dad?" I ask.
"Yeah, my cell phone doesn't work in here. But there is a phone next to your bed," Minda replies.
"I had a phone all last night?"
"Look to your left."

I try to turn my head. It hurts and won't move. Some tears roll down my cheek from the pain.

Katrina adjusts my wires and automatic bed so I am upright. The table with the phone is cantilevered. Minda positions it in front of me and holds the receiver gently to my ear and mouth. The phone is a landline with a coiled cord.

My father always answers the phone by saying "Yo." He asks if it is Minda or Mara. He wants to make me soup. I tell him I can't eat food yet. He offers to pour it down my IV.

Do I want him to visit? I tell him not at all. Next question: Am I on any good drugs? I ask Minda.

I am on morphine, steroids, and a few others I can't pronounce. My dad says morphine counts as good and gives a fifteen-minute speech. It makes me cry and laugh. It is the type of things fathers say in movies and novels before they die but uses more curse words and is funnier. He goes too far and begins to spout mouthfuls about self-destruction and how he misses my mother. I cut him off. In my sickest-sounding voice I tell him that he can't kick Eugene out. I tell him it is like the opposite of banning. My father is silent.

I call my brother Danny. I tell him I'm all right and I love him. He wants to visit. Unlike my dad, I can tell he really wants to. But I ask him not to.

I don't want anyone to visit. I'm supermoody and have wires and tubes coming out of me. There are bugs colored like candy crawling around. Sipping through a straw wears me out. My hair is thick with grease and sweat. Half of it is missing. Minda says I look like a 1920s swimmer who drowned.

My plan

Minda's cell phone can text. I send a message to Zack that I'm okay. He texts back "OMG super glad your not dead. I love U soooooo much. I promise to stop whistling when we cook."

Charlie lives on the West Coast. Minda says he won't mind waking up at 5 a.m. He is happy I've called. He wants to fly to New York. I tell him that's not necessary. "The modular origami books you wanted should be at The Store today. I wasn't sure what type. So I just got a bunch," Charlie says. I tell him thanks and we exchange I-love-yous.

"So we don't have the books here? You said you got them," I ask Minda.
"Not yet. But I have the paper. They didn't have the right books. Charlie wanted to help," she says.

I tell her I just remembered my origami plan. It was to show her and Jason how to fold the pieces. I'd get to pick the colors to fold, and put them all together. We could hang it on a string from my IV stand. "So we would be like your folding minions?" Minda assesses.
"Exactly."
She says we can do origami tomorrow. Today she has brought crossword puzzles. I want to do one but am tired.
"Take a nap. When you wake up, Jason will be here," Minda says, holding my hand.

I think I have slept. Katrina is changing my IV. She asks what pain I have on a scale of 1 to 10. I say 7 and mean it. "I can give you more morphine. It is kind of better to get off it," she advises. Katrina has spunk. She and my sister get along well. I think they would be close friends if they met another way.

Jason is sitting next to me. He has gotten sleep and is glowing. Not in the figurative sense. He is bathed in neon green light. He looks like a toy I held next to a lightbulb. I open and close my eyes till the glowing stops.

I am able to shut up today. He rests his hand on me. I hear strange noises, but am unable to turn my head to check them out. Not that I want to look away from Jason.

Dr. Zirk stops by and gives me the drunk test. My left side is still in slo-mo. I can't believe that the drunk test is not a classic children's game like thumb wrestling. It is hard to lift my legs. Dr. Zirk puts the plastic boots that inflate in waves on me. Jason is intrigued by them.

I have been given the green light to start eating certain solid foods. After three Cheerios I can eat no more. It hurts. My throat has gotten small. I ask Jason to give me five Cheerios every ten minutes so I can make it bigger. I tell him I will need blueberries for the next level. Also, I want him to give me the drunk test every hour so my left side gets better. Blueberries yes. Drunk test no.

Jason feels practicing the doctor's test is cheating. I tell him it is really more like studying and add that if I am asleep he must stockpile the Cheerios for when I wake up. Jason tells me I am too competitive and bargains me down to one drunk test a day.

I eat my five Cheerios and put on the stink cap. I'm seeing every famous black person that I've seen in my whole life. Flo-Jo. Run-DMC. Donna Summer. Richard Pryor. And so on.

"Did you have these all morning?" Jason asks.
"Yeah, pretty much. But they were less racist. Like food. Or every curtain and window treatment I've ever seen."

There is a pile of forty Cheerios waiting for me. Minda doles them out to me five at a time. By the time I finish, I need to eat five more.

"Do you want to do a puzzle?" Minda asks.

I do. She reads the clues. I answer her but am too tired to look at the grid. Normally I go faster than Minda and it is no fun, but with my handicap we have a nice volley. Jason chimes in every now and then.

This is a good crossword puzzle. The long words are all goofy homophones. 64 Across, "X to a pirate," the answer is booty mark instead of beauty mark. 17 Across—"Germy dessert to a five-year-old?"—cootie pie instead of cutie pie.

"25 down. _____ Bridge, connecting Manhattan, Queens, and the Bronx. Three letters. That's the Triborough. Should I put T-R-I in?" Minda asks.
"No. It's RFK. Put R-F-K," I say.

Minda can't believe they have changed the name, I swear to her I saw it on the way here. She says I am hallucinating until she reads "33 Across: Sasha and Malia's father." The answer is Barack and puts the *k* of *RFK* in place.

I can't take the pain anymore and am given morphine. I put on the stink mask. A swimming pool is full of milk and plain donuts. W. C. Fields is juggling the foam noodles people use for aqua aerobics.

Minda has had a powwow with Katrina. One relative is allowed to spend the night and Taylor will not be my nurse again.

Dr. Smith says I can go for short walks. A staff member must walk me. I should try to do it as often as I can to keep my legs strong.

A big woman named Monica holds my arm and supports my back. A breeze blows up my hospital gown as we walk. Our course is a lap around the nurses' station. A few of them clap for me.

We make it back to my bed. Katelyn is my night nurse. She attaches all the wires and tubes to me. I'm so tired. "You did great," Minda says. I tell her I need to walk every three hours and ask her to start a timer. I put on the stink cap and watch a parade of carpets woven with vintage restaurant names.

There is a pile of Cheerios for me to eat. Jason kisses me good-bye. He is going to Gloria's to get some sleep. I ask to walk him out.

I hold Monica's hand. We drop Jason off at the elevator. I am in uncharted waters now. Monica takes me to a window that overlooks the valet parking. I forgot about all the snow. It is stirring to watch the people down below. I want to cry but don't want Monica to think I'm soft. "The snow is pretty," I say.

"Yeah. Do you see the lights in the trees?" Monica asks.
"Yeah, are those left over from Christmas?"
"No, they are just always there."

34.

I wake up freaked out to the sounds of beeping and gasping. I've woken up like this all night. Minda has woken with me. She wakes up now, too. It is 6 a.m. We figure out how many Cheerios I need to eat.

I'm ready for blueberries. I eat five and ask that they be added to my regimen. It is time for a walk.

His name is Winston. He is older but his hands feel softer than mine. "Where you want to go?" he asks in a voice even softer than his hands.
"I'd like to see the window," I answer.
"You want the good window. It is a bit further. How you feeling?"
I tell him I can make it. We walk slowly. I stop to catch my breath. "Don't let go. This place is a maze. You let go, you never find your way back," Winston warns. We snake through hallways and double doors. We pass water fountains and waiting rooms.

Buffalo Grain Elevators, 1937, by Ralston Crawford

I almost cry, the window is large and paneless. There is a river and some factories. No billboards, no stores, nothing to pin the view to the present. "It looks just like a Ralston Crawford painting," I say in a whisper.

"I told you it was good."

We hold hands and look out the window for a long time. A really long time. Winston is waiting for me to say I want to go back. Why would I want to go back to a room without silence and windows?

"We better get back, your sister will worry," Winston says as he starts walking.

Minda helps me back into bed. Our favorite documentary film is *Poto and Cabengo*. It was made by Jean-Pierre Gorin in late 1970s California. It is about twins who have perhaps invented their own private language. The six-year-old twin girls are often subtitled with question marks. There are a few words you can make out. "Potato salad," my sister says.

"Whoopsie doo," I reply.

Jason arrives with breakfast for Minda. The smell of coffee entertains me for a solid ten minutes.

Katrina is back on call. Dr. Zirk is back too. I can lift my legs no problem. This means no more inflating leg warmers. Dr. Zirk asks how my neck is feeling.

I tell him it hurts like hell and mention that it won't turn. Dr. Zirk inspects the back of my skull and warns me that this will hurt. "Slow or fast?" he asks. "Fast," I reply.

Dr. Zirk rips something off my neck that feels like skin. He is holding a piece of crusty white tape. All of the sudden I can turn my head. It hurts, but I can see the telephone.

I celebrate with blueberries and apple juice. Jason throws the Cheerios into my mouth. I strain to catch one and accidently pull out a monitor cord. It starts beeping wildly. Jason quickly plugs it back in. Party time is over.

I'm still on the recovery floor. Recovery is a euphemism for "in a fucking bad way." There is screaming and crying. Minda is trying to get me moved to the sixth floor. She has heard from Katrina there are walls instead of curtains. I see the nurses ceaselessly ping-pong from patient to patient. I love them.

Time moves slow and is marked in Cheerios. My hallucinations are growing. I don't need the stink cap. I don't even need to close my eyes. Like my illos, they are in all different styles. It feels as though I have made a career's worth of animations. I've never taken LSD, but I understand it now. I hate it, but I get it.

The house lights are turned down. Jason departs to meet our friend Ted for an early dinner. Minda stays with me. Jason will take the night shift so Minda can go to Gloria's apartment and sleep. That is the plan.

He is younger than Winston. I request a window. He gives me the one with the hospital entrance and lights in the trees. It is still snowing. We sit down in the chairs next to stacks of magazines. The Sunday *New York Times* is spread across the coffee table. My chick-lit illustration is on the cover of the *Book Review*.

I have trouble as we walk back. I go slowly and take breaks. I can hear the noises before we enter.

Waiting to be helped into my bed I discover that the table has a drawer filled with bandages, cotton balls, and swabs that look like they haven't been touched since 1970.

Katelyn tucks me in and reconnects me. Minda asks her what the chances of me being moved today are. There is no chance.

The sounds are driving me nuts. I ask for noise-canceling head-phones. I want the good ones that yoga instructors and executives wear on airplanes. Nobody understands how badly I want these. I want them right now.

If we can't buy them we will make them. I ask Minda to riffle through the time capsule of medical supplies. A cloth bandage is wrapped around my head, securing a sanitary napkin over each ear. I look like an albino basset hound wounded in the Civil War.

Noise-canceling headphones

I make barking noises when Jason returns. He laughs so hard, I can hear him through my noise-canceling headphones. Minda is convening with Katelyn. It looks like she is getting a talking to for wasting vintage bandages.

Minda wasn't being yelled at. She was learning about a room in the corner of our floor meant to quarantine a contagious patient. Often the nurses use it to rest in. It has real walls and a door. It is mine for the night.

Minda tells me she loves me thirty times and reluctantly leaves.

Jason turns all the lights off and strokes my arm that is threaded through the railing of the bed. It is romantic. He tells me he loves me. I tell him to set an alarm for an hour. I need to grow my throat and practice the drunk test.

A warm feeling has washed over me. I wake Jason up and tell him I was in my tumor. He asks if it was a dream? I don't know. I feel amazing. It seemed so real. I try to describe everything I saw. Jason loves this story and asks me to tell it to him again. I ask why the alarm didn't go off. My throat is only one blueberry wide. We need to make it two wide by morning.

35.

Minda is having another powwow with Katrina. There is talk of them moving me to my old bed.

I have a hallucination of a screen saver made from wire-frame army guys that crawl on their elbows. The negative space somehow forms a larger army guy that then turns into a smaller army guy. I am trying to understand how it works. It is created by some sort of computer program. Jason interrupts to tell me Dr. Stieg will be visiting soon. My army guys start to mess up and vanish.

Dr. Stieg's assistant, Amanda, enters first. We are friends within five minutes. She gives me her e-mail and phone number. I can ask her questions anytime.

Babe Ruth calls me to bat. "What color is a banana? . . . Where were you born? . . . Walk in a straight line. . . . Touch your nose. . . . Touch my finger. . . . Look left. . . . Look right. . . . Very good. . . . Yes. . . . You are doing great. You are a model patient," Dr. Stieg says. Minda and Jason are beaming.

They are aching to ask questions. I don't want to waste his time. I just want his autograph. Telepathically I tell them not to bug him. It doesn't work.

"Is the tumor benign?" Jason asks.
"Oh yeah," Dr. Stieg says, like that was a waste of a question.
"Is there any chance of her being moved to the sixth floor?" Minda asks.
"Sixth floor is booked. They have you in quarantine. I guess this room works both ways. Recovery floor is tough. If I let her out, where would she go?" Dr. Stieg asks.
"Eugene's mom has an apartment a few blocks away. The plan is to go there for a little," Minda replies.

Dr. Stieg looks at me. Solid eye contact. I sweat in my pits like a tennis player.

"I'm going to discharge you. I think you will be better off there than here."

"I really get to leave today?" I ask.

"Yes. Amanda will cut your stitches out in two weeks. I'll see you in a month. Any other questions?" Dr. Stieg concludes.

"Can I hug you?" I say.

"Of course," Dr. Stieg answers.

49.

I wake up at 6 a.m. Jason is conked out. I can't go back to sleep. It is hard for me. Moments from when I was little and from when I was older. All of them cycle through me. I feel like I am backing them up in case my hard drive crashes.

This bed is so comfortable. Jason just bought it last week to replace the piece of crap we were sleeping on before. The old one was fifty dollars. We got it at a junk store run by a man named Steve. Steve had a gravelly voice and once told us Cirque du Soleil was sexy.

Jason paid a thousand dollars for our new mattress. He paid it to a guy in a white shirt and a tie at a store around the block from Gloria's while a friend babysat me because I wasn't allowed to be alone yet.

In a shallow bath I use a sea sponge to wash. I squeeze it over just the left side of my head. Minda washed me after the hospital. They stuck the monitors on my chest with the same foam mounting tape college kids use to hang pictures on the wall. She had to rub a foot exfoliant on me for an hour.

Every time my mom had a baby, my dad would bring her a lobster in the hospital. When I was born, she got two. Minda didn't bring it to the hospital because I couldn't really eat. But we ate lobster at Gloria's.

Jason is asleep behind me. My brother Charlie has sent me a link to a video of a modern Rube Goldberg machine and has asked for a photo of my scar. I send him the one Jason took at my request. Minda said it looked punk rock and I should see it. After I saw it I asked Jason to change my nickname to Baseball.

Traffic from the Brooklyn Bridge is starting to build up. I can see my bike down below chained to a pole covered in snow.

He is up! I give him a hundred little kisses. False alarm. I let him sleep.

Jason is finally awake. I'm allowed to go to the deli, where I am greeted with "Two eggs, toasted bialy."

We take the green train. Uptown feels different to me now that I've slept overnight above Fourteenth Street. Like LSD, I understand it; I don't want to do it, but I get it. Jason holds my hand when we walk. The sidewalks are slippery and I am still very weak.

There is an exhibit put on by the Grolier Club I want to see called "Lives on the Mississippi: Literature and Culture Along the Great River."

Chapbooks that describe the river's bends and early photos of cities that sprung up along the Mississippi fill the first cases. One photo depicts a city burnt to the ground, with the caption "Part of the rite of passage of a great American city in the 19th century seemed to be a great fire."

A crude map of the river has been drawn on a scroll, it's housed in a homemade box with knobs. The map scroll could be rolled back and forth as a captain floated down the river. People back then seem so clever until I think about sonar and GPS. The alarm on my phone goes off. I have set it so we won't be late to get my stitches cut out.

"This won't hurt. The nerves are dead," Amanda says, holding tweezers and bent-nosed scissors. She is wearing a coal miner's headlamp.

A week earlier there was blood in my urine. When I was released from the hospital, I was told to call Amanda if anything was wrong.

"Is it time for your period?" Amanda asked. "I wish all problems were this easy," she joked.

Amanda is standing above me now, the same way the teachers at P.S. 3 would when they checked us for lice.

"I'm just double-checking that all the stitches are out," Amanda says.
"I didn't even know you'd started," I reply.
"It's tricky because your hair is dark and the sutures are black. You know what's the worst?"
"What?"
"Asians. Their hair looks just like sutures. You don't know which is which."

The front fridge is broken, but Willie the repairman is here, so everyone is in a good mood.

My dad is in the kitchen with Zack. We sit at the counter. I close my eyes and rest my head on Jason's shoulder.

There is a ban on talking about the tumor at The Store. I don't want anyone to know, especially not art directors.

Almost as soon as we got to Gloria's duplex, my sister was sent on a run for a two-week pillbox, Dixie cups, and Marks-A-Lot fat-nib markers. Jason and I set up in the living room and began to brainstorm.

I was propped on the sofa with the three glasses of water I'd requested. Jason sat at the professional-grade grand piano. He dragged his fingers along the keys and then began playing a soulful version of Billie Joel's "New York State of Mind."

"Holy shit, when did you learn to play the piano?" I asked midsong. Jason continued to concentrate on the keys. "I can't believe this. You are so good!" I shouted. Jason looked up from the keys and smiled. He lifted his hands. The song was still going. The keys were still moving.

The sketch for the "Cooking with Dexter" illo was approved before we switched my convalescing to Brooklyn. Jason set up all the lights while I napped on the world's most comfortable mattress. The final art was e-mailed yesterday.

I'm halfway through a solo illo for *Golf Digest*. It is a quiz about the rules for moving your ball. The hard part was not hard. It felt like cement shoes were broken off. My idea of a caterpillar made from a contrail of golf balls is already approved.

My father is on his best behavior. He has not told a soul. This will not last. I called before we got here so he wouldn't ask me if the stitches were out through the pickup window. I sang the song of Amanda. He asked what was so amazing about her. I told him she shared parts of herself that nurses don't normally share, and that she lets me hug her good-bye. My dad says this is because I was split open and stripped to my core. That I could not hide who I am. How could they not expose themselves to a vulnerable jellyfish like me?

Zack walks by with a "Zackzuca." He warns the customer it is fucking hot. Zack always takes the "Zackzuca" to the table himself. Partly because he is proud and partly because it is finished with the fajita steam effect.

Tired from swallowing soup, I nuzzle my face into Jason's armpit and take a micronap. I wanted to cook brunch this weekend, but Jason dared me not to.

"Kenny, it's fixed," Willie says.
"I love you," my father replies.
Willie smiles when my father kisses and hugs him good-bye.

Picnic at Hanging Rock

ABOUT THE AUTHOR

Tamara Shopsin is a graphic designer and illustrator whose work has been featured in *The New York Times, Good, Time, Wired,* and *Newsweek.* She is the designer of the *5 Year Diary* and *Eat Me: The Food and Philosophy of Kenny Shopsin.* Two volumes of her drawings have been published under the titles *C'est le Pied!* and *C'est le Pied II.* She is a 2012 Code for America fellow and a cook at her family's restaurant in New York.

PERMISSIONS